Marriages *and* Deaths Reported *by*

DER PENNSYLVANIER

a

German Language Newspaper Published at Lebanon, Pennsylvania

1868–1879

Translated and Transcribed by

Robert A. Heilman

HERITAGE BOOKS
2009

HERITAGE BOOKS
AN IMPRINT OF HERITAGE BOOKS, INC.

Books, CDs, and more—Worldwide

For our listing of thousands of titles see our website
at
www.HeritageBooks.com

Published 2009 by
HERITAGE BOOKS, INC.
Publishing Division
100 Railroad Ave. #104
Westminster, Maryland 21157

Copyright © 2009 Robert A. Heilman

Other books by the author:

Deaths Reported by Der Libanon Demokrat, *a German Language Newspaper
Published at Lebanon, Pennsylvania, 1832–1864*

Jacob Ebersoll, the Immigrant of 1763, and His Descendants

Marriage and Death Notices Transcribed from the Pages of the Lebanon Valley Standard

Marriages Reported by Der Libanon Demokrat, *a German-Language Newspaper
Published at Lebanon, Pennsylvania*

*The Heilman Family Genealogy, Comprising Three Heilman Lines in One Volume:
John Peter Heilman (John Peter Heylman); and William B. Heilman and Their Descendants*

CD: Lebanon Valley, Pennsylvania Marriages and Deaths, 1832-1864

International Standard Book Numbers
Paperbound: 978-0-7884-5008-2
Clothbound: 978-0-7884-8206-9

Foreword

Der Pennsylvanier was a 19th century German language newspaper published at Lebanon, Pa. It was formed by the merger of the *Libanon Demokrat* and the *Berks County Zeitung,* both German language newspapers. This merger took place in May of 1865.

The paper was "published every Wednesday, simultaneously in Lebanon and Reading, Pa. at $1.50 per year payable within the year." Its Offices were located on Walnut Street in Lebanon in 1868. In 1871 the offices were at 13 South 8th Street and in 1876 the company's address was "Lock Box 8, Lebanon, Pa." The owner and publisher was John Young and Co.

Der Pennsylvanier lasted until the year 1880 when it was succeeded by another German language newspaper, *Die Volks=Zeitung,* also published at Lebanon, Pa.

Despite its 15 years of existence, few issues of this newspaper are to be found. Yet from these few issues found in the libraries of the Lebanon County Historical Society at Lebanon, Pennsylvania and the Pennsylvania State Library at Harrisburg, Pennsylvania we have a record of 256 marriages and 253 deaths that occurred more than 100 years ago in the Pennsylvania Counties of Berks, Dauphin, Lancaster, Lebanon, Lehigh and Schuylkill.

Acknowledgements

I owe a debt of gratitude to the staff of the Pennsylvania State Library for making copies of *Der Pennsylvanier* available to me and also to the staff of the Lebanon County Historical Society also for making available to me copies of *Der Pennsylvanier* from their collection of newspapers.

MARRIAGES

February 19, 1868

Lebanon County

Married. On the 13th of this month, by the Rev. F. W. Kremer, Mr. Crause McCord with Rebecca Rank, both of Lebanon.

On the 30th of January, in Lebanon, by the Rev. J. Y. Ashton, Allison T. Dickinson, of Reading, Pa., with Miss Achsah B. Brower, of Baltimore County, Maryland.

On the 23rd of January, Ferdinand Klink, of Jackson Township, Lebanon County, with Mathilde Wendling, of East Hanover, Lebanon County, Pa.

Berks County

Married. On the 19th of January, George Albright with Sarah Ann Schur, both of Exeter.

On the 25th of January, James Knecht of Reading, with Maggie Heidman of Lancaster County.

On the 8th of February, Samuel Strouse of Penn, with Catharine Schumacher of Upper Bern.

On the 8th of February, Mahlon Long with Delia Barder, both of Exeter.

On the 1st of February, Samuel Meck with Emeline Elisabeth Hertzel, both of Upper Bern.

On the 1st of February, Samuel M'Clean with Emeline Francis, both of Amityville.

On the 8th of February, Franklin Williams of Alsace, with Elisabeth Zeller of Exeter.

On the 1st of February, at the American House, Augustus Kachel of Marion, with Sarah Danbach of Womelsdorf.

On the 1st of February, William Heist with Amanda Fischer, both of Bern.

On the 8th of February, Lemuel Beidler of Spring with Caroline Troy of Brecknock.

On the 9th of February, Henrich Meck with Mary Dunlap, both of Reading.

On the 26th of January, Jacob Strauss of Penn, with Mary A. Yoh of Heidelberg.

On the 1st of February, in Womelsdorf, James W. Fidler of Marion, with Hannah Fox of Heidelberg.

November 11, 1868

Lebanon County

Married. On the 5th of November by the Rev. Steigerwalt, Dr. J. L. Mengel, of Lebanon, with Mary M. Herr, of Swatara.

On October 22, at the Evangelical parsonage, by the Rev. C. B. Brown, Edward J. Oswald and Clarissa Mondy, both of Lebanon.

On October 31st, in Jonestown, by the Rev. H. Giesz, John H. Kreiser with Sarah A. Zeller, both of Bethel Township, Lebanon County, Pa.

On the 27th of October, by the Rev. F. W. Kremer, Israel Snider, with Clara Scott, both from this city.

On the 29th of October, by the same [Rev. F. W. Kremer], Henry Lehman with Fanny Miller, both from Lancaster County.

On the same day [October 29], by the same [Rev. F. W.

Kremer], Alfred W. Bowman, of Cornwall with Sallie E. Horst, of South Lebanon Township.

On the 31st of October, by the same [Rev. F. W. Kremer], Reuben H. Hoffer, of this city, with Miss Elizabeth Bixler, of North Lebanon Township.

On the 29th of October, by the Rev. J. E. Hiester, Isaac Matternes, of Annville, with Rebecca Sattezahn, of East Hanover, Lebanon County.

On the 31st of October, by the same [Rev. J. E. Hiester], John W. Koons, with Mary Ann Strohman, both of North Annville.

On the same day [October 31], by the same [Rev. J. E. Hiester], Levi Snyder with Mary E. Houser, both from East Hanover, Lebanon County.

Berks County

Married. On the 3rd of October, Henry S. Matz of Spring, with Mary B. Keller from West Cocalico, Lancaster County.

On the 17th of October, Jacob Pott with Lusetta Bieber, both from Ontelaunee.

On the 24th of October, Charles H. Tobias with Maria H. Wensel, both of Alsace.

Some time ago, Jacob Schadler with Susan S. Baucher, both of Richmond.

On the 19th of September, Benjamin F. Shaddaow of Dauphin County, with Ellen R. Heckman, of Hamburg.

On September 25, Samuel Fries with Mary A. Miller, both of Albany.

On the 1st of October, in Allentown at Hackenbuch's Cross Key Hotel, Franklin B. Baucher of Windsor with Catharina Seider, of Hamburg.

3

On the 29th of September, John R. Borkey of Upper Bern, with Catharine B. Christi of Center.

On the 24th of October, John B. Mast of Penn, with Rebecca Elmira Reedy of Tulpehocken.

On the 31st of October, Gabriel Lutz with Sarah Ann Lengel, both of North Heidelberg.

May 11, 1871

Married. In Myerstown, on the 6th of this month, by the Rev. L. W. Craumer, R. R. Eshelman of Topton, Berks County, with Mary A. Moyer, of Myerstown, Lebanon County.

In Columbia, Pa., by the Rev. Father Peifer, William J. Schaffer of Philadelphia (formerly of Lebanon County), with Helen E. Roland, of Columbia, Pa.

In Pottsville, on the 2nd of this month, by the Rev. F. J. Pierce, Joseph E. Bruce (formerly of Lebanon) with Sallie B. Lanigan, daughter of James Lanigan, Esq., all of Pottsville.

On the 29th of April, by the Rev. Geoge Wolf, Nathaniel Line with Amanda Eisenhauer, both of Jackson Township.

June 8, 1871

Married. On the 29th of May, at the home of the bride's parents, in Hanover, by the Rev. John Binkley, Bartholomew Marquet of Lebanon, with Malinda Shugar of Hanover.

At Jonestown, on the 27th of May, by the Rev. H. Giesz, Jonathan Hershberger with Caroline Miller, both of Bethel Township, Lebanon County.

On the same day [May 27], by the same [Rev. H.

Giesz], John F. Yingst of South Lebanon Township, with Catharine F. Raudabach, of Tulpehocken Township, Berks County.

On the 3rd of May, at the same place [Jonestown], Henry Baum of Bethel Township, with Mary Fox of Swatara Township.

In Bernville, on the 27th of May, James M. Richard of Upper Bern, with Kate S. Holsman, of Tulpehocken.

On the 21st of May, Edwin M. Schollenberger of Richmond with Caroline Merkel of Spring.

On the 20th of May, Samuel Boffenmeyer with Caroline Mengel, both of Upper Bern.

On the 23rd of May, Franklin B. Davis of Bern with Lucy Ann Brenzinger of Robeson.

On the 27th of May at "Biffels Hotel," Isaac E. Pautsch with Henrietta Kline, both of Center.

June 15, 1971

Married. On the 3rd of this month, by the Rev. Abraham Pfautz, Franklin E. Hain of Bethel Township, with Hannah Bellaman of Union Township.

On the 8th of this month, by the Rev. George Wolf, C. Pease with Kate C. Bennethum, both of Reading.

On the 10th of this month, by the same [Rev. George Wolf], Elias H. Miller with Rebecca Troutman.

On the 3rd of April, Charles H. Siegfried with Ellen E. Smith, both of Hamburg.

On the 25th of April, Isaac Wise with Mary A. Breidenstein, both of Lancaster County.

June 22, 1871

Married. On the 15th of April, Peter Schadler with Mathilda Lukenild, both of Manheim, Lancaster County.

On the 3rd of this month, William H. Lengel of Upper Tulpehocken, with Rebecca E. Stamm of Penn.

On the 8th of this month, Levi S. Richard with Kate Lare, both of Jefferson.

On the 8th of June, Aaron K. Kline of Stoneville, with Mary Louisa Sands of Joanna Station.

On the 7th of this month by A. S. Ely, Esq., Samuel Hoffman with Elenora Bleistine, both of Lebanon.

July 13, 1871

Married. In Jonestown, on the 8th of this month, by the Rev. H. Giesz, Adam Peiffer of Bethel with Arah [Sarah ?] E. Hoffa of Fredericksburg.

On the 1st of this month, George Reinsel with Elmira Clauser, both of Upper Bern.

On the 1st of this month, Henry H. Hain with Sabilla C. Kalbach, both of Robeson.

On the 1st of this month, John S. Wenrich with Emma M. Zerby, both of Jefferson.

On the 1st of this month, by the Rev. Jacob Reinbold, Benjamin E. Gockley, of Elizabethtown, with Sarah A. Eberly of Heidelberg Township, Lebanon County.

In Jonestown, on the 29th of June, at the residence of the bride's parents, by the Rev. Wm. M. Reilly, Albert A. Ammerman with Emma Gelbert.

August 17, 1871

Married. On the 6th of this month, by the Rev. B. W.

Schmauk, Henry D. Fortna, with Emma L. Gebhart, both of this city.

On the 1st of August, Samuel H. Rabatt, with Catharine L. Ruth, both of West Colcalico, Lancaster County.

On the 5th of August, Emanuel G. Blatt of Jefferson with Lydia B. Seltzer of Upper Bern.

On the 5th of this month, at the residence of Monroe Moor, in this city, by the Rev. J. Dougherty, William A. Slike of Chester County, Pa., with Saville B. Mease, of Jonestown, Pa.

September 7, 1871

Married. On the 24th of August, Henry M. Sullenberger, of Penn with Henrietta E. Kleinginna of Bern.

On the 26th of August, Harriason G. Boone with Rebecca H. Price, both of Exeter.

On the 19th of July, Elias Kurtz, of Millcreek with Sarah Griffe of Heidelberg Township, Lebanon County.

On the 26th of August, William B. Wenrich of Bernville with Sarah S. Billman of Upper Bern.

On the 31st of August, Joshua Bucks of Centre with _ teria Mathilda S. Winter of Upper Bern.

On the 26th of August, Cyrus G. Batdorf with Emma Gerhart, both of Bethel, Berks County.

On the 26th of August, Jacob Peifer with Mary S. Berger, both of Bethel, Berks County.

On the 27th of August, by the Rev. George Wolf, George Dodendorf with Kate Alleman.

On the 2nd of this month, by the same [Rev. George Wolf], William Schwanger, with Elizabeth Dierwechter.

October 12, 1871

Married. On the 1st of October, Parris Stump of Greenwich, with Rebecca Reber of Orwigsburg, Schuylkill County.

On the 30th of September, Albert D. Wenrich of Upper Heidelberg with Mary M. Fischer of Heidelberg.

On the 13th of September, James Weikel with Karoline Reeser, both of Bern.

On the 30th of September, William F. Goodhart with Ellen L. Ruth, both of Reading.

On the 30th of September, Isaac Pott of Cumru with Mary Hartz of Adamstown, Lancaster County, Pa.

On the 30th of September, Henry Mose with Emma Kohl, both of Cumru.

On the 5th of October, John B. Bechtel of Birdsboro with Mary E. Geiger of Geigerstown.

On the 5th of October, Henry A. Ludwig with Clara Matz, both of Reading.

November 16, 1871

Married. On the 31st of October at Jonestown, William G. Snyder with Emma Wagner, both of West Hanover, Dauphin County.

On the 2nd of this month, at the residence of the bride's father, David H. Boeshore with Emma Porter, both of Union Township, Lebanon County.

On the 11th of this month, by the Rev. C. H. Leinbach, Jonathan Werner with Amanda Moyer, both of North Heidelberg, Berks County.

December 14, 1871

Married. On the 28th of November, Daniel Zug with Susanna Zern, both of Richmond.

On the 2nd of this month, at the home of the bride's parents, by the Rev. D. Lentz, Joseph Good with Mary Noll, both of Newmanstown, Lebanon County.

On the 11th of November, Daniel J. Moyer of Heidelberg with Sarah R. Noll of Newmanstown, Lebanon County.

On the 13th of November, the Rev. John E. Moyer with Amanda Ruth, both of Heidelberg Township.

On the 2nd of December, Mahlon Schnebely of Alsace with Malinda Messinger of Ruscumbmanor.

December 21, 1871

Married. On the 3rd of December, by the Rev. S. Noll, at the residence of the bride's mother, Israel Trump, of Dauphin County, with Amelia Feaser of Lebanon County.

On the 9th of this month, by the Rev. S. Noll, in Annville, Lebanon County, Henry J. Frank of Belleview [Bellegrove today] with Mary Howard.

In Schaefferstown, on the 16th of this month, by the Rev. J. A. Schultz, Dallas F. Walter of Lebanon with Mary C. Krum of Schaefferstown.

On the 25th of November, Percival Kilmer with Lizzie Miller, both of Myerstown, Lebanon County.

On the 6th of this month, by the Rev. B. W. Schmauk, Dr. J. H. Mease, of Lebanon, with Maria C. Gerberich, of East Hanover.

On the 25th of November, at Jonestown, by the Rev. C. H. Mutschler, Isaac Reichert, with Mary A. Zerbe, both of Schuylkill County.

On the 3rd of this month, at that place [Jonestown], by the same [Rev. C. H. Mutschler], Charles bower with Elizabeth Zieger, both of Swatara Township, Lebanon County.

On the 10th of this month, by the Rev. Charles Leinbach, Reily Dundore with Clara Ann, youngest daughter of the Rev. Thomas H. Leinbach, both of Marion, Berks County.

On the 30th of November, by the Rev. J. E. Hiester, Ammon Hess with Kate Albright, both of East Hanover.

On the 9th of this month in Jonestown, by the Rev. C. H. Mutschler, E. H. Boeshore with Elizabeth Boltz both of Fredericksburg.

April 18, 1872

Married. On the 7th of this month, in Schaefferstown, by the Rev. J. A. Schultz, T. J. Clark with C. E. Stohler, both of Philadelphia.

On the 14th of this month, by the Rev. F. W. Kremer, George R. Reis, with Carrie M. Gerhart, both of this city.

On the 19th of March, by the Rev. D. A. Laverty, Samuel A. Wallower of Harrisburg with Kate Houser of Schaefferstown.

On the 7th of this month, by the Rev. C. Leinbach, Jeremiah M. Reinhold, of Frystown, Berks County, with Harriet Eckert, of Heidelberg, Lebanon County.

On the 30th of March, in Jonestown, by the Rev. C. H. Mutschler, John Laubenstin with Mary E. Yother, both of Schuylkill County.

On the 23rd of March, by the same [Rev. C. H. Mutschler], Freeman Krepps with Kate Carver, both of Fredericksburg.

On the 6th of this month, by the same [Rev. C. H. Mutschler], Ephraim Walmer with Lizzie Nye, both of Union Township.

On the 16th, by the Rev. F. P. Mayser, John J. Miller with Sally C. Bickel, both of Jackson Township.

On the 31st of March, Daniel S. Emerich, of Reading, with Alice Heffelfinger of Bernville.

On the 30th of March, Jonathan Reis of Hamburg, with Fyette S. Loose of Upper Tulpehocken.

On the 23rd of March, Levi Zerbe with Catharine M. Moyer of Center.

On the 20th of March, John F. Filman with Sallie R. Moyer, both of Reading.

On the 23rd of March Henry Boose with Annie Radman, both of Reading.

On April 7th, Augustus S. Esterly with Annie as S. Miller, both of Reading.

July 4, 1872

Married. On the 29th of June, in Jonestown, by the Rev. H. Giesz, Adam C. Plattenberger of Cornwall, with Pryscilla Sattezahn of East Hanover.

On the 22nd of June, by the Rev. S. Noll, Jeremiah Bomgardner with Elizabeth Keller, both of Londonderry Township, Lebanon County.

On the 22nd of June, by the Rev. Henry Schropp, Samuel Asman with Elisabeth German, both of Allentown, Lehigh County.

On the 22nd of June, Henry Weidman of Perry with Emma Clouser of Shoemakersville.

On the 22nd of June, Jesse Strasser of Shoemakersville

with Sarah Roland of Reading.

On the 15th of June, Peter R. White with Mary A. Mell, both of Sinking Spring.

On the 18th of June, Henry Daum of Leesport with Caroline Stocker of Reading.

On the 29th of June, Cyrus A. Miller with Lucy M. Seaman, both of Upper Bern.

On the 29th June, Franklin Eyrich with Mary Ann Agnes, both of Bern.

July 11, 1872

Married. On the 29th of June, Hiram M. Holstein, of Millcreek with Amanda Zug of Richland.

On the 6th of this month, Edward Schell with Barbara E. Stoudt, both of Heidelberg.

On the 6th of this month, Adam J. B. Dundore with Mahella Conrad, both of Bernville.

On the 29th of June Ezra K. Levan with Susan Y. Peter, both of Oley.

On the 4th of this month, John S. Koller of Centerport with Mary Ann William of Upper Bern.

On the 6th of this month, Franklin Thompson of Reading with Hattie A. Johnson of Tamaqua, Schuylkill County.

On the 3rd of this month, by the Rev. F. W. Kremer, Charles Agin of Flemington, New Jersey, with Mary A. Regar of Cornwall.

On the 7th of this month, by the same [Rev. F. W. Kremer], William Erwin with Sarah Spang, both of Cornwall.

On the 25th of June, in Reading, by the Rev. G. Wolff, E. D. Demmy of Harrisburg with Kate Fischer of Myerstown.

On the 23rd of June, by the Rev. John Gring, Thomas W. Scherzer of Hummelstown, with Jane Loser of Bethel Township.

July 18, 1872

Married. On the 4th of this month, by the Rev. J. H. Kutz, Augustus Boyd with Lizzie Steely, both of Lebanon.

On the 30th of June, in Jonestown, by the Rev. Giesz, Michael S. Moon of Jonestown with Elizabeth Burgart, of Bethel Township.

On the 14th of this month, by the Rev. J. C. Bliem, Israel Karch with Emily M. Dundore, both of Lebanon.

On the 1st of June, Benjamin R. Hinnerschitz of Spring with E. U. Poff of Reading.

On the 11th of May, Jonathan H. Schaffer with Hannah Huffert, both of Cumru.

On the 28th of May, Solomon F. Westley with Catharine Matz, both of Cumru.

On the 8th of June, Ephraim H. Kohl with Elmina H. Mast, both of Cumru.

On the 6th of this month, Rufus Eckenroad with Elvina Fitterling, both of Cumru.

On the 15th of June, Peter N. Wheit with Mary A. Mell, both of Sinking Spring.

On the 9th of this month, by the Rev. B. W. Schmauk, William F. Hallowell with Annie R. Focht, both of Lebanon.

On the 28th of May, by the Rev. E. F. Pitcher, Frank Weidner with Annie M. Bell, both of Lebanon.

On the 29th of June, by the Rev. F. P. Mayser, Hiram Holstein of Millcreek with Amanda Zug of Richland.

On the 4th of this month, by the Rev. F. J. F. Schantz,

Napoleon B. Earnest with Mary A. Hoffer, both of Hummelstown.

On the 23rd of May, by the Rev. H. H. Gelbach, Theodore T. Taggert with Lizzie K. Mardorf, both of Lancaster County.

On the 4th of this month, by the same [Rev. H. H. Gelbach], John Honafius, of North Lebanon with Sarah E. Lape of Myerstown.

On the 7th of this month, by the Rev. C. H. Mutschler, James W. Paine with Mary B. Weber, both of Fredericksburg.

July 25, 1872

Married. On the 14th of July, by the Rev. Henry Schropp, William J. Blumer with Ellen S. Eckert, both of Allentown, Lehigh County.

On the 22nd of June, by the Rev. J. M. Dietzler, Phil. German of Annville, with Louisa Boltz of the same place.

On the 6th of July, by the same [Rev. J. M. Dietzler], Isaac Dechart with Mary A. Schott, both of Myerstown.

August 1, 1872

Married. On the 23rd of July, at the residence of Mr. Lichtenthaler, in Reading, by the Rev. Radcliff, John W. Graeff of Lebanon with Louisa M. Lichtenthaler of Reading.

On the 27th of July, John L. Kahlbach with Amanda E. Lamm, both of Robesonia.

On the 20th of July, Henry H. Killinger of Robeson with Rebecca Foose of Shoemakersville.

On the 27th of July, Francis Hemming of Spring with Catharine Dippery of Cumru.

August 8, 1872

Married. On the 27th of July, Martin Meck with Susan Hafer, both of Exeter.

On the 1st of August, Joseph Leisey of East Cocalico, Lancaster County, with Louisa Lorah of West Colcalico, Lancaster County.

On the 1st of August, James M. Phillips of Reading with Aurora Kreiter of Lititz.

On the 25th of July in Jonestown, by the Rev. C. H. Mutschler, Ephraim Darkes of Swatara, with Amanda Bressler of Bethel Township, Berks County.

On the 18th of July, by the Rev. J. E. Hiester, Jacob Brehm of West Hanover, with Amanda Shank, of East Hanover, Dauphin County.

On the same day [July 18], David Horst of South Hanover, with Kate Fackler of West Hanover, Dauphin County.

August 15, 1872

Married. On the 20th of July, by the Rev. Charles H. Leinbach, Jacob B. Boeshore of Bethel, Berks County, with Mary A. Kreiser, of Jackson.

On the 10th of this month, by the same [Rev. Charles H. Leinbach], Cyrus Smith of Bethel, Berks County, with Priscilla Martin of Swatara, Lebanon County.

On the 11th of August, George Hornefius, with Sarah R. Herbert, both of Lebanon.

On the 10th of July, Cyrus Shott, with Amelia Dreist, both of North Lebanon Township.

On the 13th of July, Edward Reyfine, with Elizabeth

Yerger.

On the 8th of August, William Greim with Mrs. Mary Umbenhauer, both of Bernville.

On the 4th of July, Charles A. Fetter, with Mary M. Yeakel, both of Elizabeth Township, Lancaster County.

On the 3rd of August, Franklin Brensinger of Long Swamp, with Sativia Dornward of Greenwich.

August 22, 1872

Married. On the 20th of July, by the Rev. Israel Hay, Daniel Feiting with Celesa Shook, both of East Hanover Township, Lebanon County.

On the 27th of July, by the Rev. C. Bucher, John W. Firestone, of Jackson, Lebanon County with Angeline Haak, of Bethel Berks County.

On the 15th of this month, by the same [Rev. C. Bucher], William Binner with Mary Schrom, both of South Lebanon.

On the 17th of August, by the same [Rev. C. Bucher], Daniel G. Conrad with Lydia W. Wann, both of Lancaster county.

On the 8th of this month, at Jonestown, by the Rev. F. J. F. Schantz, Rev. L. G. Eggers of Palmyra, with Elizabeth B. Kettering of Jonestown.

On the 19th of August, by the Rev. S. Noll, Elias Saylor, of Annville, with Mary Sourwein of Myerstown.

On the 27th of July, John P. Luff with Rebecca P. Weiser, both of Sinking Spring.

On the 27th of July, Aaron B. Reifsnyder of Sinking Spring with Henrietta R. Wisner of Bern Township.

On the 6th of August, Walter J. Seltzer with Maclada

Williams, both of Hamburg.

On the 3rd of August, James M. Moyer of Exeter with Mary Ann Olinger of Alsace.

On the 15th of August, Jacob Smith of west Cocalico, Lancaster County with Emma W. Gaul of Lower Heidelberg, Berks County.

On the 17th of August, Amandon G. Kalbach of North Heidelberg with Mary Ann Strohm of Robesonia.

August 29, 1872

Married. On the 24th of august, in the Brothers parsonage, at Allentown, by the Rev. Henry Schropp, Wilhelm Shirk with Matilda Heller, both of Mertztown, Berks County.

On the 26th of August, by the Rev. Henry S. Mutschler, Wilson Spitler with Lizzie Schreckengast, both of Union Township.

On the 8th of June, Frank Sonen of Millcreek, Lebanon County, with Kittie Ann Geltzinger, of West Cocalico, Lancaster County.

On the 8th of June, Cyrus F. Zerbe, of Womelsdorf with Hettie Hibbert of Millcreek, Lebanon County.

On the 15th of June, John Rhoads with Leah Drupple, both of Heidelberg, Lebanon County.

On the 15th of June, William Garner of Robesonia, with Isabella L. Keener, of Heidelberg.

On the 17th of August, William Fornwald of Robesonia, with Susan Rhoads of Charming Forge.

On the 17th of August, Levi Wertz with Sarah Horeman, both of Robesonia.

On the 17th of August, Joseph Herbein of Oley with Sarah Schmehl of Exeter.

September 5, 1872

Married. On the 3rd of August, Daniel Webb with Elvina Yanisch, both of Long Swamp.

On the 17th of August, Weiand Weida of Richmond with Sarah Princenhoff of Maxatawny.

On the 17th of August, Jeremiah Himmelreich with Sara Rou, both of Richmond.

Levi Strauss with Mary Ruth, both of North Heidelberg. Note: no date was given!

Allen Riegel with Sarah B. Stertzel, both of Jefferson. Again, no date was given.

On the 24th of august, William Schwambach with Sarah Kauffman, both of Leesport.

On the 29th of August, Jeremiah Strayer, Jr., with Mary Blouch, both of Lebanon.

On the 26th of August, Wilson Spitler, with Lizzie Schreckengast, both of Union Township.

On the 15th of June, John Rhoads, with Leah Drupple, both of Heidelberg.

On the 31st of August, Aaron Witmer, of Cornwall, with Mary Allwein, of North Lebanon Township.

On the 25th of August, Charles Ney, with Elizabeth Schartzer.

September 12, 1872

Married. On the 24th of August, Henry Schneider of East Cocalico, Lancaster County with Mary McCauly of Lower Heidelberg, Berks County.

On the 31st of August, Henry R. S. Haas with Sarah H.

Althaus, both of Penn.

On the 31st of August, David O. Hill with Johanna Magdalena Machemer, both of Upper Bern.

On the 3rd of September, by the Rev. J. H. Lowery, Cyrus Fernsler with Mary Moyer, both of North Lebanon.

On the 2nd of September, Tobias Reinoehl with Addie Orth, both of Lebanon.

November 28, 1872

Married. On the 3rd of this month by the Rev. Giesz, Christian Walborn of Monroe Valley with Mary K. Umberger of Jonestown.

On the 20th of this month by the same [Rev. H. Giesz], Edwin Stewart of Kleinfeltersville with Isabella Laing of Lebanon.

On the 16th of this month, Cyrus Schlessman of Bethel, Berks County with Elisabeth Krick of Bethel, Lebanon County.

On the 17th of this month, Abraham C. Seaman of Manheim, Lancaster County, with Caroline M. Miller of Bethel, Berks County.

On the 14th of this month, Reuben Hoover, with Salinda Wike, both of Lower Heidelberg.

On the 16th of this month, Aaron L. Staoudt, with Kate Spatz, both of Lower Heidelberg.

On the 16th of this month, John Whitmoyer of Reading with Elisabeth Weber of Penn.

On the 23rd of this month, by the Rev. F. W. Kremer, Jacob H. Smith of South Lebanon, with Lizzie B. Stohler of Heidelberg.

On the 16th of this month, by the Rev. B. W. Schmauk,

Nathan K. Leinaweaver of Cornwall, with Leah Moyer of Heidelberg.

At Columbus, Ohio, on the 14th of this month, at the home of the bride's parents, by the Rev. C. A. von Anda, Dr. George H. Stein, formerly of Lebanon with Ellen Lindsay.

October 1, 1874

Married. In Richland, on the 22nd of September, Dr. J. D. Zimmerman with Susan Zellers.

On the 27th of September, in Lebanon, by the Rev. F. W. Kremer, F. W. Wagner with Alice McConnell.

On the 26th of September, by the Rev. H. Giesz, C. C. Noll with Sarah Glick, both of near Mt. Zion, Lebanon County, Pa.

On the 26th of September, by the Rev. George Wolf, Joseph Siegfried of Mt. Aetna, with Barbara Miller, of Host.

On the 26th of September, by the Rev. E. S. Henry, Leonard Cooper with Rebecca Walmer, both of Fredericksburg, Lebanon County.

On the 24th of September, by the Rev. C. H. Leinbach, William Faeler of Bethel, Lebanon County, with Emma C. Swope of North Lebanon.

On the 25th of September, by the same [Rev. C. H. Leinbach], John B. Grant with Louise Hauck, both of Berks County.

On the 22nd of August, J. S. A. Schaffer, of North Heidelberg, Berks County, with Amelia H. Leininger, of Robesonia, Berks County.

On the 16th of September, S. R. Zerby of Wintersville, Berks County, with Leah Batdorf, of Tulpehocken Township.

On the 12th of September, George Schoner with Isabella

Bubb, both of Marion Township.

On the 24th of September, Adam Wenerich with Mary A. Moyer, both of Heidelberg Township.

November 23, 1876

Married. On the 16th of this month, by the Rev. F. W. Kremer, John H. Huber to Sarah Fees, daughter of Henry Fees, both of Lebanon.

On the 18th of this month, by the same [Rev. F. W. Kremer], William H. Copp of Cornwall Township with Ida M. Rhodes of Lancaster County.

On the same day [November 18], by the same [Rev. F. W. Kremer], John B. Smith of South Annville, with Susan Materness of Annville, Lebanon County.

On the same day [November 18], by the same [Rev. F. W. Kremer], Christian Yeagley with Kate Becker, both of South Lebanon Township.

On the same day [November 18], by the same [Rev. F. W. Kremer], John Dressler with Fianna Umbehend, both of this place [Lebanon].

On the 9th of this month, by the Rev. John Stamm, Philip Kettering of South Annville, with Mary Reeser of South Hanover, Dauphin County.

On the 9th of this month, by the Rev. J. E. Hiester, Henry Gruby with Catharine Garman, both of South Annville Township.

On the same day [November 9], by the same [Rev. J. E. Hiester], Alfred Eckert of South Cornwall, with Carried D. Albright of South Annville.

On the 7th of October, by the same [Rev. J. E.

21

Hiester], Albert S. Kline with Priscilla C. Bougher, both of South Annville.

On the 4th of this month, by the Rev. F. J. F. Schantz, in Myerstown, Romanus Kinckner of Norristown, with Susan S. Katzeman of Myerstown.

On the 11th of this month, by the same [Rev. F. J. F. Schantz], David S. Jones of Norristown, with Sarah R. Rothermel of Myerstown.

On the 11th of this month, by the Rev. D. D. Trexler, William Harrison Speicher with Kate A. Moser of North Heidelberg.

On the 18th of this month, by the Rev. A. S. Leinbach, Jack Miller of Ephrata, with Mary Sell of East Cocalico, Lancaster County.

November 30, 1876

Married. On the 4th of November, in Stouchsburg, Samuel H. Smith of Annville, Lebanon County, with Beckie C. Miller of Stouchsburg.

On the 11th of November, in Reading, Daniel Hatt with Annie Kuhns, both of Sinking Spring.

On the 22nd of November, Rolan Weitzel with Rose Weasenfort, both of Sinking Spring.

On the 2nd of November, Conrad D. Reber with Minnie J., daughter of James Ruth, Esq., both of Sinking Spring.

On the 4th of November, Daniel M. Seaman with Joanna A. Epler, both of Upper Bern.

On the 4th of November, Franklin Miller with Lydia K. Wagner, both of Upper Bern.

On the 23rd of this month, by the Rev. F. W. Kremer, James M. Hummel with Rebecca Shetter, both of Bismarck,

Lebanon County.

On the 4th of this month by the Rev. H. Giesz, at Jonestown, Michael Webbert of Mt. Zion with Emma Lutz, of Jackson Township.

On the same day [November 4], by the same [Rev. H. Giesz], William L. Batdorf of Greenville, with Malinda Rhoads of Marion Township, Berks County.

On the 9th of this month, by the Rev. C. H. Leinbach, John H. Stocy of Myerstown, with Clara E. Wagner of Jackson Township, Lebanon County.

On the 24th of this month, in Jonestown, by the Rev. H. Giesz, Ezekiah L. Rehrer with Selisia Bohr, both of Pinegrove Township, Lebanon County.

On the 25th of this month, by the Rev. C. Bucher, John S. Krall of Heidelberg Township, Lebanon County, with Amanda Klopp of Marion, Berks County.

On the 13th of this month, in Palmyra by the Rev. G. T. Weibel, Adam Longhouser with Mary Karl, both of South Annville, Lebanon County.

May 15, 1878

Married. On the 30th of March, by J. T. Speck, Esq., Isaac M. Kreiser with Susanna Haas, both of Union Township.

On the 4th of May, by the Rev. J. Kline, Benjamin Wagner with Sarah E. Heffner, both of Landingville.

On the 14th of this month, by the Rev. Father Kuhlman, Samuel Hartman with Miss Clara Fierer, both of Lebanon.

On the 7th of this month, by the Rev. A. M. Stirk, B. Frank Bowman with Miss Carrie Capp Bras, both of Lebanon.

On March 30th, by John H. Speck, Esq., Isaac R. Kreiser with Miss Susanna Haus, both of Union Township.

May 22, 1878

Married. On the 18th of this month, by the Rev. F. J. F. Schantz, John H. Brown of Jackson Township, Lebanon County, with Miss Catharine Binner of South Lebanon Township, Lebanon County.

On the same day [May 18], by the same [Rev. F. J. F. Schantz], John A. Weinhold with Miss Sarah M. Loeb, both of Millcreek Township, Lebanon County.

On the 9th of this month, by the same [Rev. J. F. J. Schantz], Mr. Milton H. Shaud of Jonestown with Miss Clara Sarge of Swatara Township, Lebanon County.

On the 11th of this month, by the same [Rev. F. J. F. Schantz], Reuben H. Risser with Miss Sarah C. Fees, both of Jackson Township, Lebanon County.

On the 18th of this month, by the Rev. F. W. Kremer, Aaron H. Spayd with Miss Mary A. Raybold, both of Heidelberg Township, Lebanon County.

On the same day [May 18], by the same [Rev. F. W. Kremer], George W. Light with Miss Mary A. Geib, both of South Lebanon Township.

On the 17th of this month, by the Rev. F. W. Kremer, George J. Ditzler with Miss Mary Buch, both of Lebanon.

On the 5th of May, by the Rev. J. J. Weber, Wilhelm Kohagen with Bertha Towe, both of Ashland.

On the 30th of April, in the home of the bride's parents, by the Reverends D. Sanner and G. A. Hinterleitner, Pastor Johannes Rienm (born at Winnenden Wurtemburg) of Girardsville with Josephine J. Sanner, daughter of the Rev. D. Sanner of Tremont.

On the 4th of May, by the Rev. J. R. S. Erb, Albert Lindenmuth of Landingville with Elizabeth Dretz of Cressona.

24

May 29, 1878

Married. On the 14th of May, by the Rev. F. W. Kremer, John W. Spangler with Miss Kate Lehman, both of Lebanon.

On the 23rd of May, by the Rev. M. S. Noll, George Field with Susanna Miller, both of Lebanon.

On the 23rd of May, at the residence of Edward Strickler, by the Rev. Dr. J. F. Reinmund, William R. Heilman of Jonestown, with Miss Amelia Strickler of Lebanon.

On the 23rd of May, at the residence of the bride, by the Rev. J. T. Shaffer, Mr. Jonathan J. Peters of Cornwall with Miss Sallie E. McMichael of Lebanon.

June 5, 1878

Married. On the 30th of May, by the Rev. Dr. F. W. Kremer, Jeremiah J. Boyer with Miss Mary E. Shiner, both of Cornwall.

On the 23rd of May, by the Rev. J. T. Shaffer, Thomas G. Spangler with Miss Amanda M. Light, both of Lebanon.

On the 26th of May, in Miamia County, Indiana, by the Rev. Mr. Balsbach (formerly of Dauphin County, Pa.), Mr. George Theis of Miami County, Indiana (formerly of Lebanon County, Pa.) with Mary Whisler of the above mentioned Miami County, Indiana (formerly of Lancaster County, Pa.) - born a Musselman.

On the 26th of May, in Jonestown, by the Rev. H. Giesz, Jeremiah Swope of Swatara Township with Sophia Haas of Bethel Township, Berks County.

On the 16th of May, Henry W. Hibschman of Tremont, Schuylkill County with Melinda R. Ziebach of Myerstown, Lebanon County, formerly of Bernville.

On the 18th of May, Aaron Henry Heid of Jefferson with Sarah Elizabeth Kaisee of Upper Tulpehocken.

On the 19th of May, Jacob P. Heagly with Mary C. Malone, both of Millcreek, Lebanon County.

On the 28th of May, by the Rev. Calvin Leinbach, Mr. A. Frank Eby of North Lebanon Township, with Miss Anna M. Light of Avon, Pa.

October 16, 1878

Married. On the 12th of this month, by the Rev. H. Giesz, Mr. John Webert of Mt. Zion with Miss Amanda G. Bricker of Jackson Township.

On the 1st of this month, in Miami County, Ohio, at the residence of the bride's parents, by the Rev. L. W. Schaffer, David E. Cassel of Montgomery, Ohio, with Miss Clara C. Hope of Miami County, Ohio.

On the 12th of this month by the Rev. Dr. F. W. Kremer, Reuben Brightbill, of Jonestown, this county [Lebanon], with Miss Jane E. Haack, of Cornwall Township, Lebanon County.

On the 5th of this month, by the Rev. G. J. Martz, Samuel B. Gosher with Miss Amelia E. Dierwechter, both of Heidelberg Township.

At the Tulpehocken Reformed parsonage, by the Rev. C. H. Leinbach, Franklin Edris with Miss Susan J. Spitler, both of Bethel Township. (Note: No date of marriage given.)

On the 10th of October, by the Rev. E. S. Henry, William J. Kissick of Mifflin with Clara L. Felty of Ellwood.

On the 5th of October, William Bricker of Heidelberg, with Miss Susan Beabens of Lower Heidelberg, Berks County.

On the 15th of June, in Womelsdorf, Charles H.

Bennethum of Womelsdors, Berks County with Alice L. Bennethumb of Newmanstown, Lebanon County.

On the 15th of June, in Womelsdorf, Andrew Schoener with Clara L. Anderson, both of Jefferson, Berks County.

On July 13th in Womelsdorf, Levi B. Long of Mt. Aetna with Kate A. Miller of Bethel, Berks County.

On August 10th in Womelsdorf, John H. Stahl with Emma J. Schade, both of Upper Tulpehocken, Berks County.

On August 17th in Womelsdorf, William H. Henne with Sallie M. Boltz, both of Strausstown, Berks County.

On the 24th of August, in Womelsdorf, William G. Ebling with Alice M. Reber, both of Tulpehocken, Berks County.

On the 30th of March in Womelsdorf, John W. Snader of Richland, with Sallie O. Reed of Millcreek.

On the 6th of April, in Womelsdorf, Franklin P. M. Unger of Jefferson with Arabella M. Eiler of Strausstown, Berks County.

On the 6th of April, in Womelsdorf, Daniel H. Zerbe of Strausstown with Adeline Stupp of Bethel, Berks County.

On the 18th of May, in Womelsdorf, Thomas W. Reed of Stouchsburg, with Kate Richardson of Marion, Berks County.

On the 18th of May, in Womelsdorf, Samuel Wenrich of Heidelberg, Berks County with Biianda R. Klopp of North Heidelberg, Berks County.

April 23, 1879

Married. On the 19th of this month, by the Rev. Dr. F. W. Kremer, William Christ with Anna Snyder, both of Belleview [Bellegrove], Lebanon County.

On the 8th of this month, in Jonestown, by the Rev. H. Giesz, Levi Freeman, of Bethel Township, Berks County, with Miss Lydia A. Lehman, of Bethel Township, Lebanon County.

On the 19th of this month, by the Rev. G. Wolf, Milton T. Spangler with Miss Celissa Seibert, both of Myerstown.

On the 22nd of March, in Dodge City, Kansas, by Judge Klain, Samuel R. Gingrich with Miss Clara H. Zerbe, both from Lebanon.

On the 6th of April, by the Rev. J. E. Hiester, Cyrus H. Shantz with Miss Emma L. Shenk, both of Lebanon.

On the 8th of this month, by the same [Rev. J. E. Hiester], Michael Moyer of Derry Township, Dauphin county with Miss Sue Imboden of Campbelltown, Lebanon County.

On the 14th of this month, by the Rev. A. M. Stirk, Victor E. Sarge with Miss Lizzie G. Harter, both of Lebanon.

On the 8th of this month, by the Rev. C. H. Mutschler, Samuel V. Alspach with Miss Lizzie G. Boeshore, both of Union Township.

April 23, 1879

Married. On the 8th of March, by the Rev. D. D. Trexler, James W. Greim with Emma M. Henne, both of Upper Bern, Berks County.

On the 12th of this month, by the Rev. W. F. P. Davis, Edwin M. Smith, of Fritztown, Berks County with Emma Weitmoyer, of Lower Heidelberg, Berks County.

April 30, 1879

Married. On the 22nd of March, by the Rev. M. L. Fritch, James Reppert with Maria Yost, both of Lancaster County.

On the 15th of April, by the same [Rev. M. L. Fritch], James Maurer with Jane Eckert, both of Lancaster County.

On the 26th of March, by the same [Rev. M. L. Fritch], John F. Edris, of Host, Berks County with Lizzie K. Staver, of Spring, Berks County.

On the 18th of this month, by the Rev. F. W. Kremer, Howard C. Shrack of Philadelphia with Miss Lily Hadden of this city [Lebanon].

May 7, 1879

Married. On the 4th of this month, by the Rev. F. W. Kremer, Simon G. Karch with Alice A. Behney, both of Lebanon.

On the 3rd of this month, in Reading, by the Rev. C. M. Stein, William G. Howard, of Lebanon, with Emma Stager of Reading.

June 4, 1879

Married. On the 2nd of this month, by the Rev. Dr. F. W. Kremer, Mr. Lorenzo Michael with Miss Amanda Marine, both of Lebanon.

On the 1st of this month, by the Rev. F. W. Kremer, William F. Weidle, with Miss Lizzie Barr, both of Lebanon.

On the 8th of May, by the Rev. J. G. Pfuhl, William Reindel of Harrisburg, with Maggie Hoffman, of Lebanon.

On the 20th of May, by the Rev. Charles H. Leinbach, Dr. Wilmer H. Kilmer of Myerstown with Amanda W. Kurtz of Richland.

On the 29th of May, by the Rev. G. H. Trabert, Mar. J. Shindle Krause with Miss Annie Kleiser, both of Lebanon.

On the 22nd of April, by the Rev. Dr. Kremer, George Lineweaver with Miss Fannie Buch, both of Lebanon.

On the 15th of May in North Lebanon Township, by the Rev. J. D. A. Garman, Jonas P. Moyer with Miss Mary Kessler, both of Heidelberg Township.

On the 5th of April, by the Rev. Thomas C. Leinbach, Gepperius Riegel with Fyetta K. Savage, both of Upper Bern, Berks County.

On the 17th of April, by the same [Rev. Thomas Leinbach], Franklin Beidler of Marion, Berks County, with Miss Emma R. Wilhelm of Tulpehocken, Berks County.

On the 26th of April, by the same [Rev. Thomas Leinbach], Benjamin F. Lutz with Sarah Ann Wagner, both of Jefferson, Berks County.

On the 10th of May, by the same [Rev. Thomas Leinbach], Alexander B. Unger of Penn, Berks County, with Phoebe R. Marburger of Upper Bern, Berks County.

On the 17th of May, by the same [Rev. Thomas Leinbach], at the residence of the bride, Franklin Stamm with Emma M. Geiss, both of Penn, Berks County.

On the 17th of May, by the Rev. J. H. Leinbach, Joseph Bechtel with Mary Spayd, both of Heidelberg, Berks County.

On the 18th of May by the same [Rev. J. H. Leinbach], Samuel Stamm with Mary Stamm, both of Penn, Berks County.

On the 15th of May, by the Rev. A. S. Leinbach, Cyrus W. Gaul of Heidelberg, Berks County with Mary Steffy of Spring, Berks County.

June 18, 1879

Married. On the 14th of this month, by the Rev. A.

Backman, Jacob Schenk of Schaefferstown with Kate Rutter, of Cornwall.

On the 7th of this month, by the Rev. F. W. Kremer, Andrew Loeb with Elizabeth Lewis, both of Lebanon.

On the 7th of this month, in Jonestown, William Conrad, of Ellwood, Schuylkill County, with Eliza Rupp, of Union Township.

On the 29th of May, by the Rev. C. Leinbach, Dr. Darius W. Dundore of Reading with Amanda Kurr of Rehrersburg.

On the 31st of May, Monroe G. Blatt of North Heidelberg, with Ellen H. Beckey of Marion.

August 27, 1879

Married. On the 3rd of August, by the Rev. R. Dinger, George W. Leob with Emilie Ebner, both of Raven Run, Schuylkill County.

On the 20th of this month, by the Rev. G. H. Trabert, William A. Medler of Reading, with Ella M. Arndt, daughter of Henry T. Hoffman, of Lebanon.

On the 21st of this month, by the same [Rev. G. H. Trabert], Henry Lape of Lebanon, with Emma Casser of Union Forge.

On the 9th of this month, by the same [Rev. G. H. Trabert], G. W. Sherman with Mary Danneberger, both of Jackson Township.

On the 21st of July, by the same [Rev. G. H. Trabert], Theodore Loser, with Christianna Honnefius, both of Lebanon.

On the 26th of July, by the Rev. C. Leinbach, Harrison Blatt with Mary Phillips, both of Womelsdorf.

On the 31st of July, by the same [Rev. C. Leinbach],

Thomas W. Leinbach with Martha Posy, both of Spring, Berks County.

On the 2nd of August, by the Rev. D. Davis, Ezra Kline with Eliza Zeller, both of Bethel, Berks County.

DEATHS

February 19, 1868

Lebanon County

Died. On the 10th of this month, in Lebanon, William S. Anderson, in his 40th year of life.

On the 11th of February, near Union forge, Lebanon County, Mrs. Louisa, wife of Aaron Stein, aged 30 years, 2 months and 15 days.

On the 29th of January, in Bethel Township, Berks County, widow of the late Michael Moyer, born a Boeshore, aged 7 days less than 82 years.

On the 30th of January, in Millcreek Township, Samuel Deppen, in the 72nd year of his life.

On the 13th of January 1868, in Monroe Valley, Leah J. Bucher, aged 3 years and 5 months.

On the 10th of February, Annie Lizzie, daughter of Isaac W. and Amanda Zeller, aged 5 years, 2 months and 9 days.

Berks County

Died. On the 9th of February, in Leesport, Tobias Clauser, Esq., in his 66th year of life.

On the 9th of February, at the Spring Dale Farm, near

Reading, Rebecca Deininger, in her 78th year of life.

On the 7th of February, in Reading, Mrs. Lucy L. Boyer, aged 54 years, 7 months and 7 days.

On the 2nd of February, in Lewis Township, Northumberland County, Pa., Maria, wife of Samuel Leinbach, Sr.. (born Barto), formerly of Berks County, aged 57 years, 8 months and 23 days.

On the 30th of January, in Spring, suddenly of apoplexy, Johannes Artz, aged 72 years, 2 months and 22 days.

On the 30th of January, in Windsor, of a long sickness, Daniel Bauscher, a very esteemed and influential citizen, aged 56 years.

On the 23rd of January, in Albany, of inflammation of the brain and arthritis, Ida, daughter of Benjamin and Sarah Kunkel, aged 8 months and 20 days.

On the 24th of January, in Windsor, Henry Folk, aged 78 years, 4 months and 6 days.

On the 26th of January, in Albany, of child-bed fever, Maria Elizabeth, wife of William Greenawald, born Trexler, aged 21 years, 5 months and 10 days.

On the 31st of January, in Upper Bern, of typhoid fever, Mary Jane, daughter of William and Julianna Seaman, aged 23 years, 2 months and 26 days.

On the 20th of January, near Womelsdorf, Henry Miller, aged 57 years and 14 days.

On the 26th of January, in Bern, Samuel Hartman, aged 50 years, 5 months and 10 days.

On the 6th of February, in Penn, of consumption, Peter Kerchner, aged 64 years, 10 months and 18 days.

On the 6th of February, Joseph Riegel, aged 62 years, 8 months and 6 days.

On the 24th of January, in Exeter, John Yorgy, aged 64 years, 10 months and 1 day.

On the 25th of January, in Robeson, Anna Elisabeth, daughter of Daniel and Susanna Clouser and wife of John C. Thompson, aged 23 years, 2 months and 26 days.

On the 27th of January, in Robeson, Henry Thompson, aged 75 years, 7 months and 13 days.

On the 3rd of February, in Cumru, Priscilla, daughter of Daniel and Margaret Bickel and wife of Solomon F. Westley, aged 17 years, 11 months and 15 days.

November 11, 1868

Lebanon County

Died. On the 26th of October, near Shelby, Ohio, Levi A. Kreider, formerly of Lebanon, aged 36 years.

On the 27th of October in Union Township, Ellie Louisa, daughter of Levi and Lydia Douton, aged 4 years, 7 months and 5 days.

Berks County

Died. In Earl, on the 17th of October, Isaac G. Stetler, of a kidney disorder, aged 50 years, 10 months, 14 days.

On the 13th of October, in Albany, Jacob Greenawald, aged 73 years, 7 months and 9 days.

In Richmond, on the 23rd of September, Amelia, daughter of Daniel Hoffman and Maria Hummel, aged 5 years, 3 months and 22 days.

In Richmond, on the 19th of September, Jacob, little son of Jared and Esther Wilson, aged 1 year and 9 months.

In Lenhartsville, on the 25th of September, John Jacob Steiger, aged 75 years and 13 days.

In Hamburg, on the 4th of October, Maria, wife of Samuel Schneider, aged 32 years and 18 days.

On the 16th of October, in Peik [Pike], very suddenly, Henry Diener, aged 70 years, 10 months and 4 days.

On the 12th of October, in Earl, George Dotterer, in his 68th year of life.

May 11, 1871

Died. On March 1st in Lancaster County, Susan, daughter of Edward and Sarah E. Donmoyer, aged 2 years, 1 month and 2 days.

On April 5, in Schaefferstown, Catharine, wife of Abraham Houser, aged 39 years, 9 months and 3 days.

On the 29th of April, in Lancaster County, Sabina (born Heilman), widow of the long deceased Valentine Mays, aged 88 years, 2 months and 23 days.

On the 28th of April, in Frystown, Berks County, Philip Hunsicker, aged 82 years, 1 month and 22 days. The deceased is survived by 11 children, 70 grand-children and 20 great grand-children.

On Sunday morning, the 30th of April, in Louisiana, Missouri, Mary Wilson, daughter of Frank G. and Emma A. Stickler Wilson, aged 2 years, 5 months and 4 days.

On the 24th of April, near Fredericksburg, Philip Loser, aged 49 years and 5 days.

On the 24th of April in Union Township, Jane, daughter of Philip and Esther Smith, aged 8 years, 7 months and 22 days.

On the 11th of April in Londonderry Township, Levi

Garrett, aged 50 years, 2 months and 5 days.

Near Klopp's Church, Peter Edris, aged 69 years, 7 months and 1 day. The deceased is survived by 7 children and 44 grand-children.

June 8, 1871

Died. In this city [Lebanon], on the 30th of May, Jennie M., daughter of Jonathan and Mary Reinoehl, aged 11 months. (This notice was followed by a two verse poem in English.)

In Frystown, on the 29th of May, Nathan Christ, aged 30 years, 9 months and 23 days.

In Union Township, on the 30th of May, Malinda, wife of Amos S. Ebrecht, aged 35 years, 8 months and 2 days.

In East Hanover, on the 30th of May, Adam Gerberich, aged 71 years, 11 months and 2 days.

In Hummelstown, on the 31st of May, Mary Schultz, aged 82 years.

On the 27th of May, in Cornwall Township, Emma Susan, daughter of Frederick Sprecher, aged 16 years, 9 months and 26 days.

On the 11th of May, in this city [Lebanon], of consumption, Sarah Elizabeth, wife of Ferdinand Imhoff, and daughter of Levi Smith, aged 27 years less 15 days.

On the 19th of May, in Palmyra, M. John Miller, aged 86 years, 1 month and 4 days.

On the 13th of May, in Palmyra, Louisa B. Frantz, daughter of Thomas and Barbara Frantz, aged 29 years, 9 months and 12 days.

On the 9th of May, in South Annville, George Smith, aged 64 years, 3 months and 15 days.

On the 20th of May, in Cumru, Elisa Fritz, widow of

Isaac Fritz, about 53 years old.

On the 14th of May, near Wernersville, John Yoder, husband of Elisabeth Schmehl, aged 52 years, 10 months and 18 days.

June 15, 1871

Died. In this city [Lebanon], on the 11th of this month, Bertha Ellen, child of William B. and Elizabeth Reinhard, aged 5 years, 3 months and 4 days.

In this city [Lebanon], on the 12th of this month, Elizabeth Steger, aged 51 years, 10 months and 4 days.

In South Lebanon Township, on the 7th of this month, Louisa Greib, aged 85 years, 11 months and 20 days.

In Reading, on the 10th of this month, Jacob M. Ahrens, aged 25 years, 11 months and 28 days.

June 22, 1871

Died. Near Stouchsburg, on the 19th of May, George, son of Peter and Kate Scholl, aged 2 years, 1 month and 13 days.

In Womelsdorf, on the 10th of this month, Elisabeth Glingler, aged 74 years less two days.

July 13, 1871

Died. On Monday, the 3rd of this month, in Richland, Lebanon County, at the residence of her nephew, Jacob Zug, Catharine, only daughter of the late preacher Abraham Zug who died in 1841, aged 71 years and 2 days. She was never married; she had four brothers, all of whom are still living. Her remains were interred at Royer's Meeting House in the presence of a great many people whereat the Rev. Mr. Christian Bucher delivered the funeral sermon on Galatians, 6th chapter and the last part of the 7th verse.

In Reading, on the 28th of June, Elisabeth Kisseberth, aged 59 years, 6 months and 13 days.

In Bern, on the 7th of July, Sarah McCray in the 57th year of her life.

In Jefferson, on the 31st of May, Jared Milton, aged 3 years, 8 months and 13 days.

In Jefferson, on the 17th of June, Henry Adam, aged 7 years, 4 months and 23 days. The aforementioned are children of Jared and Catharine A. Brossman.

On the 7th of this month, in this Borough [Lebanon], Jacob Siegrist, aged 62 years, 6 months and 27 days.

August 17, 1871

Died. On the 31st of July, in East Hanover Township, Lebanon County, of typhoid fever, Sarah, daughter of David and Esther Naftsinger, aged 31 years, 4 months and 5 days.

At Rehrersburg, on the 27th of July, Rebecca Peifer, daughter of Jacob and Margaretha Peifer, of cholera, aged 42 years, 4 months and 29 days.

September 7, 1871

Died. At Mt. Aetna, on the 17th of August, Joseph F. Schneider, aged 39 years 7 months and 3 days.

In Brecknock, on the 30th of August, Jacob Steffe, after an illness of 11 years, aged 67 years, 6 months and 6 days. He was buried on September 1st and the Rev. A. L. Hermann and Mennonite Preacher Ott delivered the funeral sermon in the Allegheny Church.

At Bernville, on the 15th of August, very suddenly, Adam Kauffman, aged 37 years, 7 months, 16 days.

On the 16th of August, in Millersburg, John Adam, son of Jonathan and Sarah Wolf, aged 6 years, 11 months, 7 days.

On the 9th of August, near Womelsdorf, James L. Stupp, aged 31 years, 11 months, 8 days.

On the 17th of August, in Stouchsburg, Eva Snyder, wife of Peter Snyder, aged 65 years, 6 months, 17 days.

On the 29th of July, Michael Lindemuth, of Rehrersburg, aged 79 years, 11 months, 7 days.

On the 20th of August, Solomon Emerich, of Bethel Township, aged 52 years, 2 months, 17 days.

On the 23rd of August, Lydia Bollman, of Newmanstown, aged 71 years, 6 months, 18 days.

On August 17th, in Cumru, of apoplexy, Isaac Huyett, aged 66 years, 4 months, 12 days.

On the 18th of August, in Center, of inflammation of the bowel, Joseph Grime, aged 72 years, 7 months 11 days.

On the 18th of August, in Edgerton, Johnson County, Kansas, Sarah Beckley, formerly of Myerstown.

In this city [Lebanon], on the 3rd of this month, Polly Fortna, aged 59 years, 9 months, 1 day.

In North Lebanon, on the 31st of August, Mary A. Heisy, wife of Daniel Heisy, aged 31 years, 10 months and 5 days.

On the 4th of July, in this borough [Lebanon], Catharine, wife of Elijah Langacre, aged 36 years, 9 months.

In Jackson Township, on the 3rd of August, Catharine Kissinger, aged 12 years, 2 months, 24 days.

In Hummelstown, John Parker, son of Charles D. and Elizabeth Weiss, aged 15 years, 7 months, 1 day.

On the 11th of August, in North Annville, Mara A., wife of A. H. Leslie, aged 24 years, 5 months, 23 days.

Near Fredericksburg, on the 2nd of August, Francis Joseph Mutschler (Father of the Rev. C. H. Mutschler), about 73 years old.

on the 16th of august, in Jonestown, George Washington Horn, aged 32 years, 4 months and 19 days.

On the 7th of August, in Jonestown, Catharine Rahm, wife of Henry Rahm, aged 30 years, 7 months, 8 days.

On the 12th of August, near Jonestown, Joseph Kramer, aged 6 years, 6 months.

October 12, 1871

Died. In Bern, on the 27th, Mary Schauer, wife of John Schauer, aged 72 years, 11 months, 17 days.

On the 26th of September at Heister's mill, Samuel Kercher, son of Johann and Maria (Long) Kercher, aged 77 years, 2 months, 20 days.

In Reading, on the 5th of October, the Rev. C. A. Pauli, aged 67 years, 5 months, 23 days.

November 16, 1871

Died. In Bethel, Berks County, on the 29th of October, Anna M. Eisenhauer, aged 36 years, 7 months and 24 days.

Near Leinbach's Church, on the 8th of this month, Annie Lavina, daughter of Levi and Emma Hicks, aged 9 months and 13 days.

In North Lebanon Township, on the 10th of this month, Sarah Elizabeth, daughter of Ezra and Amanda Boyer, aged 9 months and 10 days.

On the 3rd of this month, in this city [Lebanon], Rachel Wheat, aged 56 years.

On the 8th of October, in Palmyra, George R., son of John and Susan Hornketh, aged 3 years, 2 months and 16 days.

In South Lebanon, on the 12th of this month, very suddenly, Jacob Bucher, aged 64 years, 7 months and 18 days.

On the 19th of September, at her residence in Campbelltown, Sallie Schaffer, aged 71 years.

On the 25th of October, in this city [Lebanon], Grant, son of Harrison K. and Wilhelmina Dundore, aged 6 years, 2 months and 8 days.

December 14, 1871

Died. On the 3rd of November, Stricklig Wittich, son of Mr. Dietrich Wittich, of liver disease, aged 14 years and 9 months.

On the 4th of this month, in Bowmansville, Lancaster County, of typhoid fever, Caroline Becker, aged 23 years, 7 months and 24 days.

On the 6th of this month, in Upper Bern, Lydia A. Reber, aged 2 years, 11 months and 19 days.

On the 28th of November, in Upper Tulpehocken, Jacob Weible, aged 53 years, 6 months and 8 days.

On the 30th of November, near Schartelsville, Sarah Kutz, aged 48 years, 6 months and 15 days.

On the 5th of this month, Christoph Frederick Weiss, aged 84 years, 11 month and 32 days. (That's what is printed - "32 days!")

On the 25th of November, in North Annville, Mary B. Heilman, aged 77 years and 6 days.

On the 7th of this month, Bertie, daughter of William

and Sarah Wylie, aged 7 years and 4 days.

December 21, 1871

Died. In this city [Lebanon], on the 12th of this month, Cora, daughter of Anthony and Louisa Gerhart, aged 1 year, 8 months and 29 days.

On the 13th of this month, Harry L., son of James B. and Susan Miller, aged 2 years, 6 months and 10 days.

On the 8th of this month, in East Hanover, William Rider, about 73 years old.

On the 5th of this month at White Horse Station, Schuylkill County, Pa., Lodie Beaver, aged 67 years, 11 months and 5 days.

On the 10th of October in Spring, John Beidler, aged 49 years, 19 days.

On the 7th of December, near Robesonia, Elisabeth Moyer, daughter of Daniel Moyer, aged 66 years, 6 months, 15 days.

On the 9th of December in Upper Tulpehocken Township, Christophel Schaum, son of Christian Schaum and his wife who was born a Winter, aged 78 years, 10 months, 21 days. The deceased was a soldier of the War of 1812.

April 18, 1872

Died. On the 13th of this month, in this Borough [Lebanon], Elizabeth Wagner, aged 59 years, 8 months and 7 days.

In this city [Lebanon], on the 6th of this month, Jestinia Dubbs, aged 23 years, 6 months and 12 days.

On the 5th of this month, in East Hanover, Nellie Gerberich, wife of George Gerberich, aged 61 years, 11 months, 10 days.

On the 7th of this month, in North Lebanon, Leah, wife of William B. Blouch, Jr., aged 27 years, 2 months.

On the 31st of March, in Schaefferstown, Absalom Daughter, aged 72 years, 11 months, 1 day.

On the 4th of this month, near Friedensburg, Schuylkill County, John Sterner, aged 84 years, 3 months.

On the 4th of this month, in Marion, Berks County, Jacob Zeller, aged 81 years, 9 months, 26 days.

On the 31st of March in Bethel Township, Adam Miller, aged 9 years, 26 days.

On the 6th of April, in Geigertown, George Zerr, Sr., in the 84th year of life.

On the 8th of April, in Reading, George H. Ritter, Aged 7 years, 7 months, 19 days.

On the 8th of April, in Reading, of typhoid fever, Emma Schade, aged 24 year, 9 months and 15 days.

On the 13th of April, in Reading, George H. Ritter, aged 7 years, 7 months, 19 days.

On the 12th of April, in Reading, Elizabeth Higel, aged 65 years, 6 months, 6 days.

On the 29th of March, near Shoemakersville, Charles Albert Strasser, aged 5 year, 6 months, 14 days.

On the 6th of April, in Heidelberg, Anna M. Reeser, aged 58 years, 7 months, 4 days.

On the 5th of April, in Alsace, Amos Breidigam, aged 53 years, 4 months, 12 days.

On the 9th of April, in Perry, of a sore throat, Mary A. Deischer, aged 15 years, 16 days.

On the 27th of March in Mt. Zion, Lebanon County, Magdalena Webert, aged 72 years, 5 months, 10 days.

On the 31st of March, in Reading, Nathan J. Essick,

aged 18 years, 1 month, 29 days.

On the 31st of March, near Robesonia, Henry S., son of Willoughby and Sarah Becker, aged 3 years, 11 months, 5 days.

On the 21st of March, in Heidelberg, of scarlet fever, Lydia, daughter of William and Eva Good, aged 5 years, 5 months, 6 days.

On the 28th of March, in North Heidelberg, suddenly, by falling out of a tree, William Werner, aged 46 years, 16 days.

July 4, 1872

Died. On the 27th of June, in Ruscumbmanor, of consumption, Hannah Reppert, aged 69 years, 11 months, 17 days.

On the 1st of June, in Reading, Peter F. Heabner, aged 35 years, 8 months, 23 days.

On the 16th of June, in Reading, Susan Whitman, aged 49 years, 8 months, 14 days.

On the 21st of June, in Cumru, John McKinney, aged 54 years, 1 month, 6 days.

On the 19th of June, in Leesport, Susan Greenawald, aged 74 years, 5 months, 18 days.

On the 25th of June, in Reading, Anna R. Haines, aged 30 years, 1 month, 9 days.

On the 27th of June, in Reading, Moses Snyder, aged 28 years, 7 months, 15 days.

July 11, 1872

Died. On the 30th of June, in Fredericksburg, Maria Walborn, aged 77 years, 8 months and 2 days.

On the 15th of June, near the Agricultural College, Centre County, Pa., Elizabeth Meyer, formerly of South Annville Township, Lebanon County, aged 94 years, 8 months and 21 days.

On the 30th of June, near Sheridan, Isaac Person, aged 47 years, 10 months and 28 days.

On the 29th of June, in Newmanstown, Harriet Poffenberger, aged about 50 years.

On Sunday, the 30th of June, at the residence of her son, John Kochenderfer, in North Lebanon Township, widow Maria Kochenderfer, aged 81 years, 1 month and 5 days.

On the 24th of June, in Bern, of typhoid fever, William Hafer, aged 67 years, 1 month, 8 days.

On the 10th of June, in Bern, Hannah Albert, aged 67 years, 10 months, 21 days.

On the 20th of June, in Upper Bern, of an obstruction, Mahlon O. Dunkel, aged 7 years, 9 months, 7 days.

On the 1st of July, near Blandon, Adam Strunk, aged 37 years and 2 days.

July 18, 1872

Died. On the 11th of this month, of dropsy, in Jackson township, Henry Boeshore, about 81 years old.

In this city [Lebanon], on the 9th of this month, Raymond Perry, little child of Duncan and Malinda McRea, aged 3 months and 24 days.

On the 9th of this month, in North Lebanon, William H., little child of Gottlieb and Sarah Boyer, aged 5 months, 7 days.

On the 26th of June, in North Cornwall Township, Jacob Light (L. M.), aged about 70 years.

On the 31st of June, in North Lebanon, Elizabeth

Kochenderfer, aged 81 years, 1 month and 22 days.

On the 25th of May, in Reading, of typhoid fever, Mary Michael, daughter of George and Catharine Michael, aged 58 years, 1 month, 9 days.

On the 9th of this month, in Reading, Emma Wahl, aged 19 years, 7 months, 29 days.

On the 12th of this month, in Adamstown, Lancaster County, Isaac Fichthorn, aged 59 years, 6 months, 4 days.

On the 28th of June, in Hamburg, Catharine Mickley, aged 33 years, 2 months, 20 days.

On the 8th of this month, in Sinking Spring, Annie, daughter of the late William and Rebecca Gottschall, aged 1 year, 6 months, 11 days.

July 25, 1872

Died. On the 8th of July, in Windsor Castle, of dropsy, Mahlon Spears, husband of Mary Ann Rarigan, aged 46 years, 8 months, 7 days.

On the 11th of July, in Reading, Joseph Rambo (caretaker of the Rambo houses), after a brief illness of smallpox, aged 20 years, 22 days.

On the 21st of July, in Reading, Hetty Hiester, born Muhlenberg, wife of the late Dr. Isaac Hiester, in her 88th year of life.

On the 15th of this month, in Bethel Township, Elizabeth Kohr, widow of Michael Kohr, aged 89 years, 7 months and 16 days.

On the 13th of this month, Eliza Ramsey, daughter of _____ Ramsey, in South Lebanon Township, in the 21st year of life.

August 1, 1872

Died. On the 15th of July, suddenly, Patrick Maugen, aged 64 years.

On the 21st of July, Agnes Youtz, aged 2 years.

On the 28th of July, in Reading, Samuel, son of Samuel and Margaret Conner, aged 24 years, 2 months and 14 days.

On the 23 of July, William H., little child of William and Rebecca Bentz, aged 5 months and 1 day.

On the 26th, in Lebanon, Minnie Warren, daughter of Amos E. and Catharine Gans, aged 3 years, 1 month, 23 days.

On the 29th of July, Elizabeth M., daughter of Mahlon and Mary Fox, aged 10 months and 14 days.

On the 25th of July, Albert Deckert, aged 43 years, 3 months, 6 days.

On the 24th of July, in East Hanover, widow Barbara Boeshore (formerly widow Walmer), aged 84 years, 10 months and 18 days.

On the 22nd of May, in Bern, of scarlet fever, Carolina L., daughter of John and Catharina Dunkelberger, aged 1 year, 7 months and 18 days.

On the 18th of July, in Bern, of summer sicknerss, Harry, son of Jacob and Rebecca M. Rickenbach, aged 1 year, 4 months and 14 days.

August 8, 1872

Died. On the 24th of April, in Bern, of senility, widow Barbara Clemmer, aged 86 years, 11 months, 9 days.

On the 29th of July, in Heidelberg, of breast fever [pneumonia], Isabella Henrietta Klopp, daughter of Jacob and Maria Brecht and wife of William Klopp, aged 27 years, 19

(?) months and 7 days.

August 15, 1872

Died. On the 1st of this month, in Fredericksburg, Nancy Kerst, 6 years old.

On the 5th of August, in Maidencreek, Elisabeth Rothermel, wife of Paul Rothermel, aged 66 years, 2 months, 13 days.

On the 6th of August, in Muhlenberg, Susan, daughter of Joseph and Hannah Folk, 18 years old.

On the 17th of July, of senility, Philip Zerby, husband of Rosanna Lamm, aged 79 years, 5 months, 3 days.

On the 5th of August, in Womelsdorf, Amanda Lebo, aged 36 years, 2 months, 21 days.

On the 22nd of July, near White Oak, Lancaster County, of dropsy, widow Elisabeth Diem, aged 77 years, 4 months, 13 days.

On Friday of last week [August 9], Luther R. Hynicka, 4 years old.

August 22, 1872

Died. On the 14th of August, in Heidelberg, John Strohm, in the 79th years of life.

On the 12th of this month, at Greenvillage, Franklin County, Pa., Christian Oberholtzer, formerly of Fredericksburg, Lebanon County, aged 69 years, 2 months and 4 days.

On the 10th of August, in Heidelberg Township, at the residence of her son-in-law, Jacob Feierstein, widow Smith, born a Krall, aged 77 years and 16 and 1/4 hours or not a whole day over 77 years.

On the 7th of this month, in Fredericksburg, Samuel Byle, son of John Byle, aged 1 year, 3 months and 11 days.

On the 13th of this month, in Fredericksburg, William, son of William and Mary Martin, aged 6 months and 18 days.

On the 12th of this month, in Lebanon, John W., little son of John and Emma Shearer, aged 6 months and 3 days.

On the 23rd of July, in New York, James Fitzpatrick, about 25 years old.

On the 17th of this month, in Lebanon, Rosanna, daughter of Frederick and Rosanna Gardner, aged 4 years, 1 month, 19 days.

On the 17th of this month, Sabina Elizabeth, daughter of Levi and Wilhelmina Capp, aged 1 year and 9 days.

On the 19th of July, in Brecknock, Susanna Bauman, wife of Peter Bauman, aged 41 years, 4 months, 1 day.

On the 5th of August, in Robesonia, Laura Lily May, little daughter of Franklin D. and Rebecca K. Moyer, aged 3 months, 9 days.

On the 19th of July, near Sinking Spring, Mrs. Maria Ratzer, aged 77 years, 10 months, 29 days.

On the 25th of June, in Richmond, of smallpox, Catharine Becker, wife of Henry Becker, aged 66 years, 2 months, 20 days.

On the 6th of August, in Maidencreek, Susanna Kindt, wife of Samuel Kindt, aged 71 years, 3 months.

On the 2nd of August, in Bernville, James Fegley, son of Cyrus and Amelia Heffelfinger, aged 11 years, 3 months, 14 days.

On the 11th of August, in Marion, suddenly of dropsy, Leah Bickel, born Richard, aged 67 years, 6 months and 20 days.

August 29, 1872

Died. On the 19th of August, in Oley, of dysentery, Mary Kemp, widow of Daniel Kemp, aged about 71 years.

On the 13th of this month, in Lebanon, Lily Rebecca, little child of William and Rebecca Boutwell, aged 1 year, 2 months and 8 days.

On Sunday evening [August 25], in Cornwall Township, Jennie, daughter of Samuel Erb and wife.

On the 14th of this month, in Columbus, Ohio, Jacob Moore, formerly of Lebanon County, aged 74 years, 10 months and 1 day.

On the 20th of this month, in Lebanon, Frederick W., little child of Amos E. and Catharine Gantz, aged 4 years and 23 days.

On the 26th of this month, Mary A. Gockley, eldest daughter of the Sheriff of this city [Lebanon], aged 17 years, 7 months and 1 day.

On the 14th of this month, in South Annville, Milton Jerome, only child of Simon W. and Kate Bachman, aged 10 months and 14 days.

On Friday morning, the 23rd of August, in this city [Lebanon], of a brief illness, Dr. Cyrus Dorsey Gloninger, aged 48 years, 5 months and 8 days.

September 12, 1872

Died. On September 7th in Bern, of dropsy, Catharine Fischer, unmarried, aged 61 years, 6 months, 6 days.

On the 5th of September, in Womelsdorf, William Henry Mathews, aged 1 year, 4 months, 29 days.

On the 27th of August, in Exeter, Maria, wife of John

Meck, aged 50 years, 7 months, 29 days.

On the 30th of August, in Jefferson, Isaac Groff, aged 6 months, 15 days.

On the 30th of August, in Womelsdorf, of consumption, Rebecca Fidler, wife of Peter Fidler, and daughter of Adam and Harriet Valentine, aged 24 years, 4 months, 13 days.

On the 28th of August, in Bernville, Emma Blatt, aged 1 year, 2 months, 20 days.

On the 5th of September, in Cornwall Township, Charles Stewart, aged 43 years.

Pm the 5th of September, in Cornwall, Margaret Thomas, aged 66 years.

November 28, 1872

Died. On the 23rd of this month, in this city, John Musser, aged 60 years, 4 months and 19 days. His sickness was typhoid fever.

On the 23rd of October, in Fairfield County, Ohio, Maria Marburger, wife of George S. Marburger, formerly of Alsace Township, Berks County, aged 69 years, 7 months and 28 days.

On the 5th of this month, in Wernersville, Harry L., son of John and Sara Kirich, aged 4 years, 4 months and 10 days.

On the 1st of this month, in Wernersville, Katie S., daughter of Samuel and Rebecca Fischer, aged 4 years, 4 months and 7 days.

On the 14th of this month, near Stouchsburg, William H., son of William and Malinda Diehl, aged 6 years and 21 days.

On the 15th of this month, near Strausstown, Catharine, daughter of the late Jacob and Lucy Weible, aged 26 years, 11 months and __ days.

On the 26th of October, in Upper Bern, Mary Priscilla, daughter of Jacob and Sarah Rebecca Moyer, aged 3 years, 11 month and 16 days; on the 20th of October, Ida Rebecca, aged 1 year, 7 months and 7 days, twin children of the same family. All three children died of membraneous croup.

October 1, 1874

Died. On the 23rd of September, Thomas Achey, aged 75 years.

On the 16th of September, in Newmanstown, Joseph Leob, aged 55 years.

On the 7th of September in Jonestown, Hannah Crick, aged 5 years, 5 months and 4 days.

November 23, 1876

Died. On the 3rd of this month in Lebanon, Peter, son of Benjamin and Rebecca Brightbill, aged 15, years, __ months and 18 days.

In this city [Lebanon], on the 15th of this month, Mrs. Elizabeth Barto, aged 12 (?) years, 9 months and 18 days.

In this city [Lebanon], on the 15th of this month, Joseph William, child of Joseph and Harriet Lowry, aged 1 year and 4 months.

In Myerstown on the 13th of this month, Casper Sherk, aged 82 years, 10 months and 10 days.

On the 18th of November, in Reading, Jonathan L. Reber, aged 61 years and 10 months.

In Friedensburg, Berks County, November 18, David Brumbach, an old and respected citizen, in his 74th year of life.

On the 1st of November, in Penn, Berks County, David Babb, aged 51 years, 7 months, 7 days.

November 30, 1876

Died. On the 15th of October, in Bethel, Benjamin Becker, aged 58 years, 6 days.

On the 4th of November, in Jackson, John Ludwig, aged 20 years, 8 months, 24 days.

On the 9th of November, in Hamburg, Rudolph David, son of John Peter S. and Christiana (Baum) Haintz, aged 5 years, 6 months, 2 days.

On the 18th of November, in Upper Bern, following a three year affliction of nervous rheumatism and consumption, Peter Heim, husband of Hannah Berkey, aged 57 years, 6 months, 6 days.

On the 24th of this month, in Lebanon, Jacob Weaver, aged 40 years and 26 days.

On the 24th of this month, in Lebanon, Minerva, wife of James Cunningham, aged 24 years, 8 months and 20 days.

On the 18th of this month, in Lebanon, Emma Peffley, about 19 years old.

On the 15th of this month, in Lebanon, John A. M. Snavely, aged 23 years, 1 month and 27 days.

On the 16th of this month, in East Hanover, Lebanon County, Thomas Snyder, aged 22 years and 5 months.

May 15, 1878

Died. On the 18th of March, in Washington Township, Schuylkill County, of diphtheria, Magdalina, wife of Valentine

Hummel, aged 52 years and 27 days.

On the 18th of April, in North Heidelberg Township, Berks County, of putrification of the neck, Emma Alice, daughter of Amanda **G.** (?) and Anna Maria (Strohm) Kalbach, aged 5 years, 1 month and 28 days.

On April 17th, in Upper Bern, Berks County, of breast fever [pneumonia] and senility, Johannes, son of Johann and Catharine (Kaufman) Berger, aged 80 years, 1 day.

On April 22nd, in Upper Bern, Berks County, Juriah Polly, daughter of Joseph and Juriah (Dunkel) Naftzinger, of a putrid throat, aged 10 years, 11 months and 25 days.

On the 22nd of April, in Heidelberg, Berks County, of apoplexy, Catharine, widow of the late Henry Oberly and daughter of Johann and Barbara (Zeiger) Smith, aged 69 years, 2 months.

On the 25th of April, in Jefferson, Berks County, of consumption, Jacob, son of Frederick and Christina (Anspach) Blatt, and husband of Elizabeth Borkey, aged 76 years, 7 months, 5 days.

On April 21, in North Heidelberg, Berks County, Lewis Monroe, son of Jared D. and Catharine Brossman, of a sore throat, aged 7 years, 8 months, 18 days.

On the 6th of April, in Derry, Dauphin County, Daniel Strack, aged 52 years, 8 months.

May 22, 1878

Died. On the 7th of this month, in Millersburg, Berks County, Ellsworth D., son of James S. and Mary Spangler, aged 16 years, 1 month, 6 days.

On the 11th of this month, near Myerstown, George P., the little son of John R. and Susanna Fink, aged 1 year, 1 month, 22 days.

On the 16th of this month, in Myerstown, Emma R., the little daughter of Francis F. and Deliah Yost, aged 2 month, 14 days.

On the 17th of March, in Myerstown, William J., aged 7 years, and on the 18th of March, Lulor R., aged 5 years, both died of diphtheria, and were the children of Jacob and Rebecca Painter.

May 29, 1878

Died. On the 23rd of May, in Cornwall Township, Annie L., daughter of Clinton and Kate Bowman, aged 5 years, 6 months, 7 days.

On the 14th of May, in Washington Township, Sarah E., daughter of Henry L. and Catharine Zimmerman, aged 1 year, 9 months, 16 days.

On the 14th of May, in Pinegrover Township, John H., son of Philip and Rebecca Zimmerman, aged 11 years, 7 months, 5 days.

On the 21st of March, in Williamsport, Pa., Owen Moyer, formerly of Berks County, aged 57 years, 6 months, 1 day.

On the 26th of May, in Lebanon, Ella, daughter of James Hummel, aged 22 years, 6 months, 20 days. Her funeral took place today (Wednesday) before noon at the First Reformed Church.

On the 22nd of May, in Lebanon, Dr. Jacob Hittell, aged 80 years, 10 months, 28 days.

On the 23rd of May, in Lebanon, Carl W., son of William H. and Clara Snyder, aged 5 years, 9 months, 9 days.

June 5, 1878

Died. On the 17th of May, in Lancaster, Pa., Amos Rhoads, formerly of Lebanon, 65 years old.

On the 10th of May, in North Heidelberg, of consumption, Fietta Rebecca, daughter of Daniel and Rebecca (Gruber) Bickel, aged 17 years, 9 months, 1 day.

On the 2nd of May, in Bern, of a putrid throat, Beulah, daughter of Samuel S. and Emma L. (Miller) Hetrick, aged 5 years, 8 months, 17 days.

On the 2nd of May, in Heidelberg, of consumption, Sarah Anna, wife of Johann Bennethum, and daughter of Daniel and Maria (Leininger) Kunius, aged 33 years, 22 days.

On the 14th of May, in Jefferson, of a putrid throat, Lora Loanna, daughter of Samuel Pierce and Mary Anna (Moyer) Aulenbach, aged 2 years, 4 months, 26 days.

On the 15th of May, in Upper Bern, of senility, Jacob Epler, son of Adam and Margaretha (Schlappig) Epler and widower of the late Margaretha Bowman, aged 80 years, 11 months, 8 days.

On the 4th of this month, in Lebanon, Simon, son of William C. Fauber, in his 9th year of life.

October 16, 1878

Died. On the 18th of September, in Bern, Berks County, Deborah Lovina, aged 3 years, 7 months, 22 days - on the 23rd of September, James Monroe, aged 6 years, 9 months, 17 days - on the 27th of September, Jennie Rebecca, aged 5 years less a few hours - all children of John and Maria (Roth) Binkley. All of them died from diphtheria.

On the 1st of this month, near New Ringold, Schuylkill

county, Mrs. Jonathan Yost, wife of the late Jonathan Yost in the 76th year of life.

On the 28th of September, in Pottsville, Schuylkill County, buried in Pinegrove, Precilla, wife of Henry Aulsh, aged 33 years and 28 days.

On the 2nd of this month, in West Brunswick, Schuylkill county (near Auburn), Peter Mengel, aged 56 years and 5 months,

On the 9th of this month, in Lebanon, Emma, daughter of Joseph Mann, aged 16 years.

On the 6th of this month, in Millcreek Township, John Zellers, aged 79 years.

On the 17th of July, in Womelsdorf, Berks County, Catharine, widow of the late Daniel Kalbach, aged 78 years, 8 months and 28 days.

On the 8th of August, in Marion, Berks County, Sarah Jane, daughter of Franklin and Sarah (Smith) Rhine, aged 10 months, 24 days.

On the 18th of July, in Womelsdorf, Berks County, Bertha May, daughter of Levi and Mary Bennethum Wise, aged 9 months, 20 days.

On September 14th, in Stouchsburg, Katie, daughter of Henry W. and Rebecca (Moyer) Cooper, aged 9 months, 21 days.

On September 16th, in Schaefferstown, Lebanon County, Sarah Susanna (Holtzman), wife of Reuben Kaufman, aged 26 years, 7 months, 23 days.

On the 17th of September, in Womelsdorf, Berks County, John Irvin Elmer, son of Tobias H. and Margaret Neff, aged 9 years, 8 months, 18 days.

On the 18th of September, in Robesonia, Elizabeth (Rader), wife of Jacob Wenrich, aged 73 years, 2 months and

25 days.

On the 20th of September, in North Heidelberg, Berks County, Wilson Thomas, son of John J. and Sarah Fidler, aged 2 years, 6 months, 24 days.

On the 22nd of September, in the same place [North Heidelberg], Edwin Relson, son of John K. and Sarah Fidler, aged 8 years, 10 months, 24 days.

April 23, 1879

Died. **Near Leinbach's Church, on the 9th of this month, Henry Brecht, aged 79 years, 2 months and 26 days.**

In Lebanon, on the 18th of this month, Miss Sarah Louser, aged 72 years, 3 months and 4 days.

In Lebanon, on the 29th of this month, T. F., only son of T. S. and Lydia Walmer, aged 3 years, 6 months and 8 days.

In Lebanon, on the 20th of this month, Mrs. Precilla Urban.

In Lebanon, on the 19th of this month, Mrs., wife of Samuel Treist, Jr.

In Lebanon, on the 10th of this month, Mrs. Catharine Hornberger, wife of William Hornberger, aged 41 years, 4 months and 4 days.

In Lebanon, on the 14th of this month, of heart disease and dropsy, Edward White, about 48 years old.

In Jonestown, on the 9th of this month, John Kaley, aged 84 years, 2 months and 1 day.

Near Bernville, Berks County, on the 26th of March, Joseph Manbeck, aged 78 years, 6 months, 22 days.

In Bethel, Berks County, on the 1st of this month, John Werth, aged 58 years, 2 months and 12 days.

In the Lebanon County almshouse, on the 7th of April, Julian Yeiser, aged 66 years, 10 months, 12 days.

In Shartelsville, Berks County, on the 15th of March, Harry F., son of Joseph and Kate (Fox) Burkhart, aged 48 years, 4 months and 30 days.

In Millersburg, Berks County, on the 27th of March, Frank Geyer, husband of Rebecca Holtzman, aged 26 years, 1 month, 2 days.

In Orwigsburg, Schuylkill County, on the 10th of April, the Rev. Samuel Gaumer, aged 72 years, 7 months and 9 days.

Near Richland, last week, Daniel Schaup, aged 69 years, 8 months and 26 days.

Not far from Womelsdorf, last week, Peter Herzog, very suddenly of heart disease, in his 65 year of life.

April 30, 1879

Died. Near Richland, on the 8th of this month, Daniel Shoup, aged 69 years, 8 months and 29 days.

Near Schaefferstown, on the 15th of this month, William Crist, aged 76 years, 8 months and 26 days.

In Newmanstown, on the 24th of this month, Mrs. James Wallace (born Hippert), aged 69 years and 9 months.

In South Lebanon Township, on Thursday morning [April 24], Jacob Spangler, shoemaker, about 70 years old.

In Pinegrove Township, Schuylkill county, on the 7th of April, Minnie Alice, daughter of Alfred and Sarah Kentner, aged 1 years, 3 months and 1 day.

In Mahanoy Plane, Schuylkill County, on April the 13th, Susan, wife of John C. Zimmerman, aged 43 years, 11 months and 16 days.

In Pinegrove, Schuylkill County, on the 19th of April,

John A. Baar, aged 18 years, 4 months and 9 days.

In Lebanon County, on the 8th of April, Daniel Schaub, son of the late John Schaub, formerly of Cumru Township, Berks County, aged 69 years, 8 months and 29 days.

In Spring, Berks County, on the 22nd of February, of a heart attack, Peter Krick, aged 73 years, 4 months and 7 days.

In Spring, Berks County, on the 12th of April, Jacob Maurer, aged 51 years, 8 months and 12 days.

In Brecknock, Berks County, on the 13th of April, Joseph Steffy, aged 70 years, 1 month and 7 days.

May 7, 1879

Died. In Lebanon, on the 23rd, Israel H., son of George and Rebecca Karch, aged 28 years, 1 month and 23 days.

In the Independent District, on the 29th of April, Harrison Keller, aged 35 years and 13 days.

In his residence, near Masi__on [Massilon], Ohio, on the 12th of April, Levi Foltz, formerly of Lebanon County, aged 52 years and 4 months.

Near Richland, on the 8th of April, Daniel Shoup, aged 69 years, 8 months and 29 days.

Near Schaefferstown, on the 15th of April, William Crist, aged 76 years, 8 months and 29 days.

In Spring, Berks County, on the 1st of April, Catharine, daughter of Samuel and Hanna Reifsnyder, wife of Samuel B. Becker, aged 33 years and 16 days.

In Berks County, on the 3rd of April, Elizabeth, daughter of George and Anna Maria Haag, wife of John Kleinginne, aged 54 years, 8 months and 15 days.

June 4, 1879

Died. In Lebanon, on the 27th of May, Amelia Forney, aged 62 years, 2 months and 8 days.

In Lebanon, on the 25th of May, Annie B., daughter of Reuben and Anna Wenrich, aged 19 years, 11 months and 22 days.

In Lebanon, on the 30th of May, Susan A. Shirk, daughter of the late Col. William Shirk, aged 43 years, 4 months and 15 days.

On the 11th of May, in Upper Bern, Berks county, of child-bed fever and gangrene, Maria Magdalena Miller, daughter of Jacob and Hannah (Balthaser) Renno, and wife of Moses L. Miller, at the age of 35 years, 9 months and 20 days.

June 18, 1879

Died. On the 8th of June, near Smithville, Wayne County, Ohio, George Schuey, aged 75 years, 11 months and 6 days. His sickness was dropsy.

In Bethel, Berks County, on the 27th of May, John Snyder, aged 81 years, 2 months and 7 days.

In Philadelphia, on the 11th of this month, Emma Sebina, daughter of Benjamin Mace and wife of _____ , aged 41 years, 1 month and 12 days. The funeral took place at Schaefferstown.

In Lewistown, Pa., on the 29th of May, Michael Fichthorn, aged 70 years.

August 27, 1879

Died. In Marion, Berks County, on the 9th of this month, Catharine, wife of Henry Midenfort, aged 55 years, 6 months,

5 days.

In Lewistown, Schuylkill County, on the 9th of this month, Sarah Yentzer, wife of Jeremiah Yentzer, aged 54 years, 2 months and 9 days.

In Ashland, Schuylkill County, on the 29th of July, Johann Christian Herald, aged 53 years, 1 month and 18 days.

In Porter Township, Schuylkill County, Ella Cora, little daughter of John Shall, aged 1 year and 3 days.

In Lebanon, on the 21st of this month, Christopher Rutter, son of C. W. and Susan Carmany, aged 1 year and 20 days.

In Lebanon, on the 18th of this month, Jacob Heisey, aged 76 years.

Index

Beidler, Lemuel- 2
Bell, Annie M.- 13
Bellaman, Hannah- 5
Bennethum, Alice- 27
Bennethum, Charles- 27
Bennethum, Kate C.- 5
Bennethum, Johann- 56
Bennethum, Sarah Anna- 56
Bentz, Rebecca- 47
Bentz- William - 47
Bentz, William H.- 47
Berger, Catharine Kaufman - 54
Berger, Johann - 54
Berger, Johannes- 54
Berger, Mary S.- 7
Berkey, Hanna- 53
Bickel, Daniel- 34, 56
Bickel, Fietta Rebecca- 56
Bickel, Leah- 49
Bickel, Margaret- 34
Bickel, Priscilla- 34
Bickel, Rebecca- 56
Bickel, Sally C.- 11
Bieber, Lusetta- 3
Billman, Sarah S.- 7
Binkley, Deborah Lavina- 56
Binkley, James Monroe- 56
Binkley, Jennie Rebecca- 56
Binkley, John- 56
Binkley, Maria- 56
Binner, Catharine- 24
Binner, William- 16
Bixler, Elizabeth- 3
Blatt, Christina Anspach - 54
Blatt, Emanuel G..- 7
Blatt, Emma- 51
Blatt, Frederick- 54
Blatt, Harrison- 31
Blatt, Jacob- 54
Blatt, Monroe G.- 31
Bleistine, Elenora - 6
Blouch, Leah- 43
Blouch, Mary- 18
Blouch, William B.- 43
Blumer, William J.- 14
Boeshore, Barbara- 47
Boeshore, David H.- 8
Boeshore, E. H.- 10
Boeshore, Henry- 45
Boeshore, Jacob- 15
Boeshore, Lizzie G.- 28
Boffenmeyer, Samuel- 5
Bohr, Selisia- 23
Boltz, Elizabeth- 10
Boltz, Louisa- 14
Boltz, Sallie M.- 27
Boone, Harrison G.- 8
Boose, Henry- 11

Borkey, John R.- 4
Boutwell, Lily Rebecca- 50
Boutwell, Rebecca- 50
Boutwell, William- 50
Bower, Charles - 10
Bowman, Alfred W.- 3
Bowman, Annie L.- 55
Bowman, Clinton- 55
Bowman, Frank- 23
Bowman, Kate- 55
Bowman, Margaretha- 56
Boyd, Augustus- 13
Boyer, Amanda- 40
Boyer, Ezra- 40
Boyer, Gottlieb- 45
Boyer, Jeremiah- 25
Boyer, Sarah- 45
Boyer, Sarah Elizabeth -
40
Boyer, William H.- 45
Bras, Carrie Capp- 23
Brecht, Henry- 58
Brecht, Jacob- 47
Breeht, Maria- 47
Brehm, Jacob- 15
Breidenstein, Mary A.- 5
Breidigam, Amos- 43
Brensinger, Franklin- 16
Brenzinger, Mary Ann- 5
Bressler, Amanda- 15
Bricker, William- 26
Brightbill, Benjamin- 52

Brightbill, Peter- 52
Brightbill, Rebecca- 52
Brightbill, Reuben- 26
Bollman, Lydia- 39
Brossman, Catharine- 38,
54
Brossman, Henry Adam-
38
Brossman, Jared- 38
Brossman, Jared D.- 54
Brossman, Jared Milton-
38
Brossman, Lewis Monroe-
54
Brower, Achsah B.- 1
Brown, John H.-24
Bruce, Joseph E.- 4
Brumbach, David- 52
Buch, Fannie- 30
Buch, Mary- 24
Bucher, Christian- 38
Bucher, Jacob- 41
Bucher, Leah J.- 32
Bucks, Joshua- 7
Burgart, Elizabeth- 13
Burkhart, Harry F.- 59
Burkhart, Joseph- 59
Burkhart, Kate Fox- 59
Byle, John- 49
Byle, Samuel- 48

C

Capp, Sabina Elisabeth- 49

Capp, Levi- 49

Capp, Wilhelmina- 49

Carmany, Christopher- 62

Carmany, C. W.- 62

Carmany, Susan- 62

Carver, Kate- 10

Cassel, David E.- 26

Casser, Emma- 31

Christi, Catharine- 4

Christ, Nathan- 36

Christ, William- 27

Clark, T. J.- 10

Clauser, Elmira- 6

Clauser, Tobias- 32

Clemmer, Barbara- 47

Clouser, Anna Elisabeth- 34

Clouser, Daniel- 34

Clouser, Emma- 11

Clouser, Susanna- 34

Conrad, Daniel G.- 16

Conrad, Maybella- 12

Conrad, William- 31

Conner, Margaret- 47

Conner, Samuel- 47

Cooper, Henry- 57

Cooper, Katie- 57

Cooper, Leonard- 20

Cooper, Rebecca Meyer- 57

Copp, William H.- 21

Crick, Hannah- 52

Crick, William- 60

Crist, William- 59

Cunningham, James- 53

Cunningham, Minerva- 53

D

Danbacher, Sarah- 2

Darkes, Ephraim- 15

Daughter, Absalom- 43

Daum, Henry- 12

Davis, Franklin B.- 5

Dechert, Albert- 47

Dechert, Isaac- 14

Deischer, Mary A.- 43

Demmy, E. D.- 12

Deppen, Samuel- 32

Dickinson, Allison- 1

Diehl, Malinda- 51

Diehl, William- 51

Diehl, William H.- 51

Diem, Elisabeth- 48

Diener, Henry- 35

Dierwechter, Amelia E.- 26

Dierwechter, Elizabeth- 7

Dippery, Catharine- 14

Ditzler, George H.- 24

Dodendorf, George- 7

Donmoyer, Edward- 35

Donmoyer, Sarah- 35
Donmoyer, Susan- 35
Donneberger, Mary- 31
Donton, Ellie Louisa- 34
Donton, Levi- 34
Donton, Lydia- 34
Dornward, Sativia- 16
Dotterer, George- 35
Dreist, Amelia- 15
Dressler, John-21
Dretz, Elizabeth- 24
Drupple, Leah- 17, 18
Dubbs, Jestinia- 42
Dundore, Adam J. B.- 12
Dundore, Darius W.- 31
Dundore, Emily M.- 13
Dundore, Grant- 41
Dundore, Harrison K.- 41
Dundore, Reily- 10
Dundore, Wilhelmina- 41
Dunkel, Mahlon O.- 45
Dunkelberger, Carolina L. - 47
Dunkelberger, Catharine- 47
Dunkelberger, John- 47
Dunlap, Mary- 2

E

Earnest, Napoleon B.- 14
Eberly, Sarah A.- 6

Ebling, William G.- 27
Ebner, Emilie- 31
Ebrecht, Amos S.- 36
Ebrecht, Mary Malinda- 36
Eby, A. Frank- 26
Eckenroad, Rufus- 13
Eckert, Alfred- 21
Eckert, Ellen S.- 14
Eckert, Harriet- 10
Eckert, Jane- 29
Edris, Franklin- 26
Edris, John F.- 29
Edris, Peter- 36
Eggers, L. E.- 16
Eiler, Arabella M.- 27
Eisenhauer, Amanda- 4
Eisenhauer, Anna M.- 40
Emerich, Daniel- 11
Emerich, Solomon- 39
Epler, Adam- 56
Epler, Jacob- 56
Epler, Joanna A.- 22
Epler, Margaretha- 56
Erb, Jennie- 50
Erb, Samuel- 50
Erwin, William- 12
Eshelman, R. R.- 4
Essick, Nathan J.- 43
Esterly, Augustus- 11
Eyrich, Franklin- 12

F

Fackler, Kate- 15
Fackler, William- 20
Fackler, William- 20
Fauber, Simon- 56
Fauber, William C.- 56
Feaser, Amelia- 9
Fees, Sarah 21
Fees, Sarah C.- 24
Fegley, James- 49
Feierstein, Jacob- 48
Feiting, Daniel- 16
Felty, Clara L.- 26
Fernsler, Cyrus- 19
Fetter, Charles A.- 16
Fichthorn, Isaac- 46
Fichthorn, Michael- 61
Fidler, Edwin Relson- 58
Fidler, James- 2
Fidler, John J.- 58
Fidler, John K.- 58
Fidler, Peter- 51
Fidler, Rebecca- 51
Fidler, Sarah- 58
Fidler, Wilson Thomas- 58
Field, Georg- 25
Fierer, Clara- 23
Filman, John F.- 11
Fink, George P.- 54
Fink, John R.- 54
Fink, Susanna- 54

Firestone, John W.- 16
Fischer, Amanda- 2
Fischer, Kate- 12
Fischer, Katie- 51
Fischer, Mary M.- 8
Fischer, Rebecca- 51
Fischer, Samuel- 51
Fitzpatrick, James- 49
Fitterling, Elvina- 13
Focht, Annie B.- 13
Folk, Hannah- 48
Folk, Joseph- 48
Folk, Susan- 48
Foltz, Levi- 60
Foose, Rebecca- 14
Forney, Amelia- 61
Fornwald, William- 17
Fortna, Henry D.- 7
Fortna, Polly- 39
Fox, Elizabeth M.- 47
Fox, Hannah- 2
Fox, Mahlon- 47
Fox, Mary- 5, 47
Francis, Emeline- 1 (2)
Frank, Henry J.- 9
Frantz, Barbara- 36
Frantz, Louisa B.- 36
Frantz, Thomas- 36
Freeman, Levi- 28
Fries, Samuel- 3
Fritz, Elisa- 36
Fritz, Isaac- 37

G

Gant, AmosE.- 47
Gant, Catharine- 47
Gant, Minnie Warren- 47
Gardner, Frederick- 49
Gardner, Rosanna- 49
Garman, Catharine- 21
Garner, William- 17
Garrett, Levi- 36
Gaul, Cyrus W.- 30
Gaul, Emma W.- 17
Gaummer, Samuel- 59
Geib, Mary A.- 24
Geiger, Mary E.- 8
Geiss, Emma M.- 30
Gelbert, Emma- 6
Geltzingder, Kittie Ann- 17
Gerberich, Adam - 36
Gerberich, George- 42
Gerberich, Nellie- 42
Gerberich, Maria V.- 9
Gerhart, Anthony- 42
Gerhart, Cora- 42
Gerhart, Emma - 7
Gerhart, Emma L. - 7
Gerhart, Louisa - 42
German, Elisabeth - 11
German, Phil - 14
Geyer, Frank - 59
Gingrich, Samuel A. - 28

Glick, Sarah - 20
Glingler, Elisabeth - 37
Gockley, Benjamin. - 6
Good, Eva- 44
Good, Joseph - 9
Good, Lydia - 44
Good, William - 44
Goodhart, William S. - 8
Goshen, Samuel B. - 26
Gottschall, Annie - 46
Gottschall, Rebecca - 46
Gottschall, William - 46
Graeff, John W. - 14
Grant, John B.-20
Greenawald, Jacob- 34
Greenawald, Susan- 44
Greib, Louisa- 37
Greim, William- 16
Griffe, Sarah- 7
Grim, James W.- 28
Grime, Joseph- 39
Groff, Isaac- 51
Gruby, Henry- 21

H

Haag, Anna Maria- 60
Haag, Elizabeth- 60
Haag, George- 60
Haag, Jane- 26
Haak,Angeline- 16
Haas, Henry R. S.- 18

Haas, Sophia- 25
Haas, Susanna- 23
Hadden, Lily- 29
Hafer, Susan- 15
Hafer, William- 45
Hain, Franklin E.- 5
Hain, Henry- 6
Haines, Anna- 44
Haintz, Christiana- 53
Haintz, John Peter- 53
Haintz, Rudolph David- 53
Hallowell, William F.- 13
Harter, Lizzie G.- 28
Hartman, Samuel- 23, 33
Hartz, Mary- 8
Hatt, Daniel- 22
Hauck, Louise-20
Heabner, Peter F.- 44
Heagly, Sarah P.- 26
Heckman, Ellen R.- 3
Heffelfinger, Amelia- 49
Heffelfinger, Alice- 11
Heffelfinger, Cyrus- 49
Heffner, Sarah E.- 23
Hehny, William H.- 27
Heid, Aaron Henry- 26
Heidman, Maggie- 1
Heilman, Mary B.- 41
Heilman, Sabina- 35
Heilman, William R.- 25
Heim, Peter- 53

Heisey, Jacob- 62
Heisy, Daniel- 39
Heisy, Mary A.- 39
Heist, William- 2
Hemming, Francis- 14
Henne, Emma M.- 28
Herald, John Christian- 62
Herbert, Sarah R.- 15
Hershberger, Jonathan- 4
Herr, Mary M.- 2
Herzog, Peter- 50
Hess, Ammon- 10
Hetrick, Beulah- 56
Hetrick, Emma L.- 56
Hetrick, Samuel- 56
Hibbert, Hettie- 17
Hibschman, Henry W. - 25
Hicks, Annie Lavina- 40
Hicks, Emma- 40
Hicks, Levi- 40
Hiester, Isaac - 46
Higel, Elizabeth - 43
Hill, David O. - 19
Himmelreich, Jeremiah - 18
Hiinnershitz, Benjamin R. - 13
Hittell, Jacob - 55
Hoffa, Ara - 6
Hoffer, Hannah - 13

Kalbach, Sabilla- 6
Kaley, john- 58
Karl, Mary- 23
Karch, George- 60
Karch, Jared H.- 60
Karch, Israel- 13
Karch, Rebecca-60
Karch, Simon G.- 29
Kaufman, Reuben- 57
Kaufman, Sarah Susanna- 57
Kauffman, Adam- 39
Kauffman, Sarah- 18
Keener, Isabella L.- 17
Keller, Elizabeth- 11
Keller, Harrison- 60
Keller, John S.- 12
Keller, Mary B. - 3
Keller, Matilda - 17
Kemp, Daniel - 50
Kemp, Mary - 50
Kentner, Alfred - 59
Kentner, Minnie Alice - 59
Kentner, Sarah - 59
Kercher, Johann - 40
Kercher, Maria Long - 40
Kercher, Samuel - 40
Kerchner, Peter - 33
Kerst, Nancy - 48
Kessler, Mary - 30
Kettering, Elizabeth - 16

Kettering, Philip - 21
Kindt, Samuel - 49
Kindt, Susanna - 49
Killinger, Henry H. - 14
Kilmer, Percival - 9
Kilmer, Wilmer H.- 29
Kinckner, Romanus- 22
Kirich, Harry L.- 51
Kirich, John- 51
Kirich, Sara- 51
Kissick, William J.- 26
Kisseberth, Elisabeth- 38
Kissinger, Catharine- 39
Kleinginna, Henrietta C. - 7
Kleiser, Annie- 29
Kline, Aaron K.- 6
Kline, Albert- 22
Kline, Ezra- 32
Kline, Henrietta- 5
Klink, Ferdinand K.- 1
Klopp, Amanda- 23
Klopp, Biianda R.- 27
Klopp, Isabella Henrietta - 47
Klopp, William- 47
Knecht, James- 1
Kochenderfer, Elizabeth - 46
Kochenderfer, John- 45
Kochenderfer, Maria- 45
Kohl, Emma- 8

Lindenmuth, Albert- 24
Lindenmuth, Michael- 39
Line, Nathaniel- 4
Lineweaver, George- 30
Loeb, Andrew- 31
Loeb, George W.- 31
Loeb, Joseph- 52
Loeb, Sarah M.- 24
Long, Levi R.- 27
Long, Mahlon- 1
Longhouser, Adam- 23
Loose, Fyette S.- 11
Lorah, Louisa- 15
Loser, Jane- 13
Loser, Philip- 35
Loser, Theodore- 31
Louser, Sarah- 58
Lowry, Harriet- 52
Lowry, Joseph- 52
Lowry, Joseph William- 52
Ludwig, Henry A.- 8
Ludwig, John- 53
Luff, John A.- 16
Lukenild, Mathilde- 6
Lutz, Benjamin F.- 30
Lutz, Emma- 23
Lutz, Gabriel- 4

M

Mace, Benjamin- 61

Mace, Emma Sebina- 61
Machemer, Johanna Magdalena- 19
Malone, Mary C.- 26
Manbeck, Joseph- 58
Mann, Emma- 57
Mann, Joseph- 57
Marburger, George- 51
Marburger, Maria- 51
Marburger, Phoebe R.- 30
Mardorf, Lizzie K.- 14
Marine, Amanda- 29
Marquet, Bartholomew- 4
Martin, Mary- 48
Martin, Priscilla- 15
Martin, William- 49
Mast, Elmina H.- 13
Mast, John R.- 4
Materness, Susan- 21
Matterness, Isaac- 3
Matz, Catharine- 13
Matz, Clara- 8
Matz, Henry S.- 3
Maugen, Patrick- 47
Maurer, Jacob- 60
Maurer, James- 29
Mays, Valentine- 35
McCauly, Mary- 18
McCord, Crause- 1
M'Clean, Samuel- 1
McConnell, Alice- 20
McCray, Sarah- 38

McMichael, Sallie E.- 25
McRea, Duncan- 45
McRea, Malinda- 45
McRea, Raymond Perry- 45
Mease, J. H.- 9
Mease, Savilla B.- 7
Meck, Henrich - 2
Meck, John - 51
Meck, Maria - 51
Meck, Martin - 15
Meck, Samuel - 1
Medler, William A. -31
Mell, Mary A. - 12, 13
Mengel, Caroline - 5
Mengel, J. L. - 2
Mengel, Peter - 57
Merkel, Caroline - 5
Messinger, Malinda - 9
Meyer, Elizabeth - 45
Michael, Catharine - 46
Michael, George - 46
Michael, Lorenzo - 29
Michael, Mary - 46
Mickley, Catharine - 46
Midenfort, Catharine - 61
Midenfort, Henry - 61
Miller, Adam- 43
Miller, Annie S.- 11
Miller, Barbara- 20
Miller, Beckie C.- 22
Miller, Caroline- 4

Miller, Caroline A.- 12
Miller, Caroline M.- 19
Miller, Eliza H.- 5
Miller, Fanny- 2
Miller, Franklin- 22
Miller, Hannah Balthaser - 61
Miller, Harry L.- 42
Miller, Jack- 22
Miller, Jacob- 61
Miller, James R.- 42
Miller, John- 11
Miller, Kate- 27
Miller, Lizzie- 9
Miller, Maria Magdalena- 61
Miller, Mary A.- 3
Miller, M. John- 36
Miller, Susan- 42
Miller, Susanna- 25
Mondy, Clarissa- 2
Moon, Michael S.- 13
Moor, Monroe- 7
Mose, Henry- 8
Moser, Kate A.- 22
Moyer, Amanda- 8
Moyer, Catharine M.- 11
Moyer, Daniel- 9, 42
Moyer, Elisabeth- 42
Moyer, Franklin D.- 49
Moyer, Ida Rebecca- 52
Moyer, Jacob- 52

Moyer, James M.- 17
Moyer, John E.- 9
Moyer, Jonas- 30
Moyer, Laura Lily May- 49
Moyer, Leah- 20
Moyer, Mary- 19
Moyer, Mary A.- 4, 21
Moyer, Mary Priscilla- 52
Moyer, Michael - 28, 32
Moyer, Owen- 55
Moyer, Rebecca K.- 49
Moyer, Sallie A.- 11
Moyer, Sarah Rebecca- 52
Muhlenberg, Hetty- 46
Musseer, John- 51
Mutschler, C. H.- 40
Mutwchler, Francis Joseph - 40

N

Naftsinger, Daniel- 38
Naftsinger, Esther- 38
Naftsinger, Sarah- 38
Naftzinger, Joseph- 54
Naftzinger, Juriah Dunkel - 54
Naftzinger, Juriah Polly - 54
Neff, John Irwin- 57
Neff, Margaret- 57

Neff, Tobias H.- 57
Noll, C. C.- 20
Noll, Mary- 9
Noll, Sarah- 9
Nye, Charles- 18
Nye, Lizzie- 11

O

Oberholtzer, Christian- 48
Oberly, Catharine,- 54
Oberly, Henry- 54
Olinger, Mary Ann- 17
Oswald, Edward S.- 2
Orth, Addie- 19

P

Paine, James W.- 14
Painter, Jacob- 55
Painter, Lulor R.- 55
Painter, Rebecca- 55
Painter, William- 55
Parker, Charles D.- 39
Parker, John- 39
Pauli, C. A.- 40
Pautsch, Isaac B.- 5
Pease, C.- 5
Peifer, Jacob- 7, 38
Peifer, Margaret- 38
Peifer, Rebecca- 38
Peiffer, Adam- 6

Peffley, Emma- 53
Person, Isaac- 45
Peter, Susan Y.- 12
Peters, Jonathan J.- 25
Phillips, James- 15
Phillips, Mary- 31
Pierce, Samuel- 56
Plattenberger, Adam C.-
11
Poff,E. U.- 13
Poffenberger, Harriet- 45
Porter, Emma- 8
Posy- 32
Pott, Isaac- 8
Pott, Jacob- 3
Price, Rebecca H.- 7
Princenhoff, Sarah- 18

R

Rabatt, Samuel H.- 7
Radman, Annie- 11
Rahm, Catharine- 40
Rahm, Henry- 40
Rambo, Joseph- 46
Ramsey, Eliza- 46
Rank, Rebecca- 1
Rarigan, Mary Ann- 46
Ratzer, Maria- 49
Rau, Sara- 18
Raudabach, Catharine- 5
Raybold, Mary A.- 24

Reber, Alice M.- 27
Reber, Conrad D.- 22
Reber, Ezekial- 23
Reber, Jonathan- 52
Reber, Lydia- 41
Reber, Rebecca- 8
Reed, Sallie O.- 27
Reed, Thomas W.- 27
Reedy, Rebecca Elmira- 4
Regar, Mary A.- 12
Reeser, Anna M.- 43
Reeser, Karoline- 8
Reeser, Mary- 21
Reichert, Isaac- 9
Reindel, William- 29
Reifsnyder, Aaron- 16
Reifsnyder, Catharine- 60
Reifsnyder, Hanna- 60
Reifsnyder, Samuel- 60
Reinbold, Jeremiah- 10
Reinhard, Barbara Ellen-
37
Reinhard, Elizabeth- 37
Reinhard, William B.- 37
Reinoehl, Jennie- 36
Reinoehl, Jonathan- 36
Reinoehl, Mary- 36
Reinoehl, Tobias- 19
Reis, George R.- 10
Reis, Jonathan- 11
Reinsel, George- 6
Reppert, Hannah- 44

Reppert, James- 28
Reyfine, Edward- 15
Rhine, Franklin- 57
Rhine, Sarah Jane- 57
Rhine, Sarah Smith- 57
Rhoads, Amos- 56
Rhoads, John- 17, 18
Rhoads, Malinda- 23
Rhoads, Susan- 17
Rhodes, Ida M.- 21
Rickenbach, Harry- 47
Rickenbach, Jacob- 47
Rickenbach, Rebecca- 47
Richard, James M.- 5
Richard, Leah- 49
Richard, Levi S.- 6
Richardson, Kate- 27
Rider, William- 42
Riegel, Allen- 18
Riegel, Germerius- 30
Riegel, Joseph- 33
Rienm, Johannes- 24
Ritter, George H.- 43
Risser, Reuben A.- 24
Roland, Helen E.- 4
Roland, Sarah- 12
Rothermel, Elisabeth- 48
Rothermel, Paul- 48
Rothermel, Sarah R.- 22
Rupp, Eliza- 31
Ruhl, Isabella- 21
Ruth, Amanda- 9

Ruth, Catharine- 7
Ruth, Ellen L.- 8
Ruth, Mary- 18
Ruth, Minnie- 22
Rutter, Kate- 31

S

Sands, Mary Louisa - 6
Sanner, D. - 24
Sanner, Josephine - 24
Sarge, Clara - 24
Sarge, Victor E. - 28
Sattezahn, Pryscilla - 11
Sattezahn, Rebecca - 3
Savage, Fyetta K. - 30
Saylor, Elias - 16
Schade, Emma - 27, 43
Schadler, Peter - 6
Schaffer, Jonathan - 13
Schaffer, J. S. A. - 20
Schaffer, William T.- 4
Schartzer, Elizabeth - 18
Schaub, Danniel- 60,
Schauer, John - 40
Schauer, Mary - 40
Schaum, Christina - 42
Schaum, Christopher - 42
Schaup, Daniel - 59
Schell, Edward - 12
Schenk, Jacob - 31
Scherzer, Thomas - 13

Schlessman, Cyrus - 19
Schmehl, Elisabeth - 37
Schmehl, Sarah - 17
Schnebely, Mahlon - 9
Schneider, Henry - 18
Schneider, Jacob e. - 38
Schneider, Maria - 35
Schneider, Samuel - 35
Schoener, Andrew- 27
Scholl, George - 37
Scholl, Kate - 37
Scholl, Peter - 37
Schollenberger, Edwin M. - 5
Schoner, George - 20
Schott, Mary A.- 14
schrack, Howard C. - 29
Schrackengast, Lizzie - 17, 18
Schram, Mary - 16
Schuey, George - 61
Schultz, Mary 36
Schumacher, Catharine - 1
Schur, Sarah Ann - 1
Schwanbach, William - 18, 18
Schwanger, William - 7
Scott, Clara - 2
Seaman, Abraham - 19
Seaman, Daniel M. - 22
Seaman, Lucy M. - 12

Seibert, Celisa - 28
Seider, Catharina - 3
Sell, Mary - 22
Seltzer, Lydia b.- 7
Seltzer, Walter - 16
Shaddow, Benjamin F. - 3
Shadler, Jacob - 3
Shaffer, Sallie - 41
Shall, Ella Cora - 62
Shall, John - 62
Shank, Amanda - 15
Shantz, Cyrus H. - 28
Shaud, Milton H. - 24
Shearer, Emma - 49
Shearer, John - 49
Shearer, John W. - 49
Shenk, Emma - 28
Sherk, Casper - 52
Sherman, G. W. - 31
Shetter, Rebecca - 22
Shiner, Mary E. - 25
Shirk, Susanna - 61
Shirk, Wilhelm - 17
Shirk, William - 61
Shook, Celesa - 16
Shott, Cyrus - 15
Shoup, Daniel-59, 60
Shugar, Malinda - 4
Siegfried, Charles - 5
Siegfried, Joseph - 20
Siegrist, Jacob - 38
Slike, William A. - 7

Smith, Barbara Zeiger - 54

Smith, Cyrus - 15

Smith, Edwin M. - 28

Smith, Ellen E. - 5

Smith, Esther - 35

Smith, George - 36

Smith. Jacob - 17

Smith, Jacob H. - 19

Smith, Jane - 35

Smith, Johann - 54

Smith, John B.- 20

smith, Levi - 36

Smith, Philip - 35

Smith, Samuel- 22

Snader, John W. - 27

Snavely, John A. M.- 53

Snider, Israel - 2

Snyder, Anna - 27

Snyder, Carl W.- 55

Snyder, Clara - 55

Snyder, Eva - 39

Snyder, John - 61

Snyder, Levi - 3

Snyder, Moses - 44

Snyder, Peter - 39

Snyder, Thomas - 53

Snyder, William G.- 8

Snyder, William H. - 55

Sonen, Frank - 17

Sourwein, Mary - 16

Spang, Sarah - 12

Spangler, Elisabeth D. - 54

Spangler, Isaac - 59

Spangler, James S. - 54

Spangler, John W. - 25

Spangler, Mary - 54

Spangler, Milton T. - 28

Spangler, Thomas - 25

Spatz, Kate - 19

Spayd, Aaron H. -24

Spayd, Mary - 30

Spears, Mahlon - 46

Speicher, William Harrison - 22

Spitler, Susan J. - 26

Spitler, Wilson - 17, 18

Sprecher, Emma Susan - 36

Sprecher, Frederick - 36

Stager, Emma- 29

Stahl, John H. - 27

Stahler, C. E. - 10

Stamm, Franklin - 30

Stamm, Mary - 30

Stamm, Rebecca C. - 6

Stamm, Samuel - 30

Staver, Lizzie K. - 29

Steely, Lizzie - 13

Steffe, Jacob - 38

Steffy, Joseph - 60

Steffy, Mary - 30

Steger, Elizabeth - 37

Steiger, John Jacob - 35
Stein, Aaron - 32
Stein, George H. - 20
Stein, Louisa - 32
Stertzel, Sarah A. - 18
Stetler, Isaac G.- 34
Stetner, John - 43
Stewart, Charles - 51
Stewart, Edwin - 19
Stocker, Caroline - 12
Stohler, Lizzie B.- 19
Story, John H. = 23
Stoudt, Aaron L. - 19
Stoudt, Barbara E. - 12
Strack, Daniel - 54
Strassen, Jesse - 11
Strasser, Charles Albert - 43
Strause, Jacob - 2
Strause, Levi - 18
Strayer, Jeremiah - 18
Strickler, Amelia - 25
Strickler, Edward - 25
Strohm, John - 48
Strohm, Mary Ann - 17
Strohman, Mary Ann - 3
Strouse, Samuel - 1
Strunk, Adam - 45
Stump, Parris - 8
Stupp, Adeline - 27
Stupp, James L. -39
Sullenberger, Henry M. -

7
Swope, Emma- 20
Swope, Emma C.- 20
Swope, Jeremiah - 25

T

Taggert, Theidire T.- 14
Theis, George - 25
Tobias, Charles H. - 3
Thomas, Margaret - 51
Thompson, Franklin - 12
Thompson, Henry - 34
Thompson, John C.- 34
Tome, Bertha - 24
Treist, Samuel Jr. - 58
Troutman, Rebecca - 5
Troy, Caroline - 2
Trump, Israel - 9

U

Umbenhauer, Mary - 16
Umbehend, Fianna -21
Umberger, Mary K. - 19
Unger, Alexander B. - 30
Unger, Franklin P. M. - 27
Urban, Precilla - 58

V

Valentine, Adam-51
Valentine, Harriet - 51

W

Wagner, Benjamin- 23
Wagner, Clara E.- 23
Wagner, Elizabeth- 42
Wagner, Emma - 8
Wagner, F. W. - 20
Wagner, Lydia - 22
Wagner, Sarah Ann - 30
Walborn, Christian - 19
Walborn, Maria - 44
Wahl, Emma - 46
Wallace, James - 59
Wallower, Samuel A. - 10
Walmer, Barbara - 47
Walmer, Ephraim - 11
Walmer, Lydia - 58
Walmer, Rebecca - 20
Walmer, T. F.- 58
Walmer, T. J.- 58
Walter, Dallas K.- 9
Wann, Lydia W. - 16
Weasenfort, Rose - 22
Weaver, Jacob - 53
Webb, Daniel - 18
Webbert, Michael, 23
Weber, Elisabeth - 19
Weber, Mary B. - 14
Webert, John - 26

Webert, Magdalena - 43
Weible, Catharine - 51
Weible, Jacob - 41, 51
Weible, Lucy - 51
Weida, Weiand - 18
Weidle, William F.- 29
Weidman, Henry - 11
Weidner, Frank - 13
Weikel, James - 8
Weinhold, John A.- 24
Weiser, Christoph
Frederick - 41
Weiser, Rebecca - 16
Weitmoyer, Emma - 28
Weitzel, Rolan - 22
Wendling, Mathilde - 1
Wenrich, Adam - 21
Wenrich, Albert D. - 8
Wenrich, Anna - 61
Wenrich, Anna B.=- 61
Wenrich, Elizabeth - 57
Wenrich, Jacob - 57
Wenrich, John S. - 6
Wenrich, Reuben - 61
Wenrich, Samuel - 27
Wenrich, William B.- 7
Wensel, Maria H. - 3
Werner, Jonathan - 8
Werner, William - 44
Werth, John - 58
Wertz, Levi - 17
Westley, Simon F.- 34

Westley, Solomon E. - 13
Wheat, Rachel - 41
Wheit, Peter N.- 13
Whisler, Mary - 25
white, Edward- 68
White, Peter R. - 12
Whitman, Susan - 44
Wike, Salinda - 19
Wilhelm, Emma R. - 30
William, Mary Ann - 12
Williams, Francis - 1
Williams, Maclada - 17
Wilson, Emma A. Srickler - 35
Wilson, Esther - 34
Wilson, Frank G. - 35
Wilson, Jared - 34
Wilson, Jacob - 34
Wilson, Mary - 35
Winter, Mathilde - 7
Wisner, Henrietta - 16
Wise, Bertha - 57
Wise, Isaac -5
Wise, Levi - 57
Wise, Mary Bennethum - 57
Witmer, Aaron - 18
Wittich, Dietrich - 41
Wittich, Stricklig - 41
Wolf, John Adam - 39
Wolf, Jonathan - 39
Wolf, Sarah - 39

Wylie, Bertie - 42
Wylie, Sarah - 42
Wylie, William - 42

Y

Yanisch, Elvina - 18
Yeagley, Christian - 21
Yeakel, Mary M. - 16
Yeiser, Julian - 59
Yentzer, Jeremiah - 62
Yentzer, Sarah - 62
Yerger, Elizabeth - 16
Yingst, John F. - 5
Yoder, John - 37
Yoh, Mary A. - 2
Yorgey, John - 34
Yost, Delilah - 55
Yost, Emma R. - 55
Yost, Francis F.- 55
Yost, Jonathan - 57
Yost, Maria - 28
Yother, Mary E. - 10
Youtz, Agnes - 47

Z

Zeller, Amanda - 32
Zeller, Annie Lizzie - 32
Zeller, Elisabeth - 1
Zeller, Eliza - 32
Zeller, Isaac - 32

Zeller, Jacob - 43
Zeller, Sarah A. - 2
Zellers, John - 57
Zellers, Susan - 20
Zerber, Clara A. - 28
Zerbe, Cyrus F. - 17
Zerbe, David H. - 27
Zerbe, Levi - 11
Zerbe, Mary A. - 9
Zerby, Emma M. - 6
Zerby, Philip - 48
Zerby, S. R. - 30
Zern, Susanna - 9
Zerr, George Sr. - 43
Ziebach, Melinda A. - 25
Zieger, Elizabeth - 10
Zimmerman, Catharine - 55
Zimmerman, Henry - 55
Zimmerman, J. D. - 20
Zimmerman, John A. - 55
Zimmerman, John C.- 59
Zimmerman, Philip - 55
Zimmerman, Rebecca - 55
Zimmerman, Sarah - 59
Zimmerman, Sarah E. - 55
Zug, Abraham - 37
Zug, Amanda - 12
Zug, Catharine - 37
Zug, Daniel -9
Zug, Jacob - 37

www.ingramcontent.com/pod-product-compliance
Lightning Source LLC
Chambersburg PA
CBHW070901280326
41934CB00008B/1539